THE RISE OF ENGLISH STUDIES

UNIVERSITY OF HULL PUBLICATIONS

THE RISE OF
ENGLISH STUDIES

An Account of the
Study of English Language and Literature
from its Origins to the
Making of the Oxford English School

D. J. PALMER

Published for the UNIVERSITY OF HULL *by the*
OXFORD UNIVERSITY PRESS
LONDON   NEW YORK   TORONTO
1965

Oxford University Press, Amen House, London E.C.4

GLASGOW NEW YORK TORONTO MELBOURNE WELLINGTON
BOMBAY CALCUTTA MADRAS KARACHI LAHORE DACCA
CAPE TOWN SALISBURY NAIROBI IBADAN
KUALA LUMPUR HONG KONG

© *University of Hull 1965*

PRINTED IN GREAT BRITAIN IN THE CITY OF OXFORD AT THE ALDEN PRESS

MANY of the Graces of Poetry may, I grant, be talk'd of in very intelligible Language, but intelligible only to those who have a natural *Taste* for it, or are born with a Talent of judging. To have what we call *Taste*, is having, one may say, a new Sense or Faculty superadded to the ordinary ones of the Soul, the Prerogative of fine Spirits! and to go about to pedagogue a Man into this sort of Knowledge, who has not the Seeds of it in himself, is the same thing as if one should endeavour to teach an Art of seeing without Eyes.

—L. Welsted, *Dissertation concerning the Perfection of the English Language and the State of Poetry*, 1724.

PREFACE

THIS is not a complete history of English studies, but an attempt to show why and how our language and literature have become subjects of academic study. The process was long and at times fiercely resisted, for the study of English in England began in quite a humble and informal way, as a kind of poor man's Classics, and more than a hundred years passed before it won recognition as a branch of scholarship in the highest seats of learning. I have illustrated the assumptions and attitudes which gave direction and increasing importance to the subject throughout the nineteenth century: in a complex of social and educational change, the missionaries of culture and the proliferating examination system between them fostered a subject of unprecedented popularity, but its developing possibilities and pleasures were stunted for want of proper academic standards and of trained teachers. The progress of the subject through these early phases is reflected in the recruitment of its first professors; originally most of them came from the Low Church or Dissenting Ministry, then from journalism, and later from the Oxford 'Greats' School, particularly from Balliol. After a series of pitched battles and tactical evasions, the Oxford English School was founded in 1894, to demonstrate that the academic study of English, properly conceived, was neither 'mere chatter about Shelley' nor 'mere philology', and to organize the training of those scholars who would promote English studies in the new civic universities. This task was left to Oxford, while for several years to come, the older linguistic Tripos in Cambridge obstructed the introduction there of a school with literary interests. The establishment of a School of English in the home of 'Greats' was a decisive challenge to the long supremacy of classical studies, for the small group of men who created the Oxford School believed that the study of English language and literature not only deserved but now needed to draw upon the traditions and resources of the ancient university. It was their achievement to secure the advent of English studies as a

Preface

fully-developed branch of humane learning, and in that sense the making of the Oxford English School is the final and most important episode in this story.

In an earlier form, this study was prepared as a thesis for the B.Litt. at Oxford, and I was fortunate enough to have my work supervised by the late Professor F. P. Wilson. I am also indebted to Mr. John Buxton, of New College, Oxford, for his encouragement and advice; to Professor Kathleen Tillotson, of Bedford College, London, for the information and assistance she gave at the start of this study; and to Miss Helen Gardner, of St. Hilda's College, Oxford, for the criticisms and suggestions which she and the late Professor Nichol Smith offered when examining my thesis. I am also grateful to my colleagues in the English Department, University of Hull, Mr. C. B. Cox, who read certain chapters in draft, and Professor R. L. Brett, who gave generously of his time to save me from errors large and small. To my wife, who assisted me at all stages and who prepared the Index, I owe particular thanks.

CONTENTS

CONTENTS

I

RHETORIC AND BELLES LETTRES

THE academic study of English literature, as we know it in schools and universities, has developed within the last hundred and fifty years. During that time, it has emerged from humble and informal origins to become a subject of central importance in orthodox English education. Yet it has never finally settled down, or been allowed to take itself for granted: well-worn controversies about the scope and purpose of the subject perennially divide those engaged in teaching it, and in certain quarters it is still suspiciously regarded as an occupation not altogether respectable, good neither for education nor for literature. Of their very nature, English studies resist arbitrary definition, and consequently retain some curious features: if the subject 'just growed', its history has been more complex and more extensive than that of most other academic disciplines. Therefore, to understand the forces which have promoted and determined the emergence of English studies, we have to go back into currents of social and literary history, before the study of English literature, with its now traditional affiliations, ultimately acquired a name and status of its own.

There is a natural point of departure in the last quarter of the sixteenth century, when Englishmen first became conscious of their own national literature. The achievements of the Elizabethan poets were recognized by their contemporaries as contributions to a kind of corporate enterprise, by which the English language was made eloquent, 'mightily enriched, and gorgeouslie invested in rare ornaments and resplendent abiliments', as Francis Meres wrote in 1598. The sense of national pride is felt, too, by George Puttenham, congratulating the poets who had 'so much beautified our English tong as at this day it will be found our nation is nothing inferior to the French or Italian'. These critics voiced the general feeling in their awareness of the new vernacular literature as a national possession.[1] If they regarded literature as the hand-maiden of language, this was a natural state of affairs, for the endeavours of the poets arose from a faith in the potentialities of the vernacular, and a desire to adapt it as a vehicle fit for the learning and eloquence which they so much admired in the ancient languages, and emulated in the Italian and French. Earlier in the century, confidence in the vernacular had been asserted, though more defensively, by humanist scholars and translators such as Sir Thomas Elyot, Sir Thomas Hoby, and William Tyn-dale, whose work was animated by the desire to educate, to reach an unlearned audience. These attitudes towards the English langu-age therefore preceded and conditioned the conscious endeavours of the Elizabethan poets, in particular of Sidney and Spenser, to bring an English literature into being. Awareness of the language anticipated awareness of the literature. So the Elizabethans looked back to Chaucer as the well of English, and Spenser's homage was followed in 1598 by Thomas Speght's edition and commentary, which in its treatment of Chaucer as a classic may be accounted the first service of scholarship to the transmission of English literature. We begin our history here, not so much because Eng-lish literature was created anew in the sixteenth century, but be-cause the Elizabethans thought it was: from this time the English were aware of their own literary culture.

Even though that same admiration of classical learning, which inspired the humanist interest in the vernacular, effectively pre-cluded the introduction of English into the educational curriculum, nevertheless the exclusively literary education of humanist ideals has a relevance for us, because the methods and principles of teach-ing Latin, Greek, or Hebrew were eventually to be adapted to the study of English.

The chief aim of a sixteenth-century grammar school was to train its pupils to speak and write correct classical Latin, an ideal which endured for another two centuries.[2] Developed from the medieval school curriculum of the *trivium*, rhetoric and logic were

[1] R. F. Jones, *The Triumph of the English Language*, Stanford, 1953, p. 179 *et passim*.
[2] The most detailed information about English grammar schools in the sixteenth century is to be found in T. W. Baldwin, *William Shakespere's Small Latine & Lesse Greeke*, 2 vols., Urbana, 1944. See also J. Foster Watson, *The English Grammar Schools to 1660*, 1908.

very closely related in the methods of analysis and composition; and according to the precepts of Erasmus and his disciple Colet, who re-founded St. Paul's School in 1509, grammar also was not to be taught separately, but alongside the reading of texts. Roger Ascham, similarly, recommended that syntax should be learned through translating and retranslating Cicero, rather than through studying a grammar-book by itself: 'for without doute, *Grammatica* it selfe, is sooner and surer learned by examples of good authors, than by naked rewles of *Grammarians*'.[3] But the rules of accidence were the first steps that had to be learnt before much reading or writing could be done. The Latin *Grammar* compiled by William Lily, the first High Master of St. Paul's School, was prescribed for use in all grammar schools. Reading involved construing, parsing, and memorizing, while spoken Latin was learned from Terence and from the 'colloquies' specially composed as text-books. Written Latin, after the elementary stage of translating 'vulgars', or English sentences, was learned by imitation, in the composition of epistles of various kinds, or themes, or, in the highest forms, verse composition. The aim of the exercises in composition was not to convey information or express original views, but to elaborate some commonplace by means of the various devices prescribed in the rhetorical handbooks. In the seventeenth century, Greek and Hebrew were not unusual attainments for a pupil in the higher forms of a grammar school, but the hallmark of his classical scholarship was his ability in composing Latin and Greek verses. And in the eighteenth century, with the final decline of Latin as a living language, this classical education lost whatever utilitarian purpose it once had, and became more literary: Greek verse advanced as Latin prose was neglected.

From grammar school to university, the student passed from a study of the ancient languages to a study of the knowledge embodied in those languages. At least during his first year, however, rhetoric would still occupy his attention, and his undergraduate studies in logic and moral philosophy were directed towards a close scrutiny of the classical texts prescribed, rather than to a discursive treatment of the subjects themselves. Humanist enthusiasm

---

[3] R. Ascham, *The Scholemaster* (1570), ed. W. A. Wright, 1904, p. 259.

for the ancients strengthened the role of the Arts Faculty: Ascham, for example, advocated the cultivation of languages and philosophy for their own sakes, distinct from the subsequent studies in the other three faculties of divinity, law, and medicine. But here, too, studies were devoted to the ancient authorities, particularly to the Greeks. Aristotle remained entrenched at Oxford, even as late as the eighteenth century, when Cambridge had introduced Locke and Newton into the syllabus, and had replaced logic with mathematics. Thus, to use Erasmus's distinction between the study of 'words' and 'things', education in the grammar schools and the universities was almost wholly literary, and classical.[4]

Within the scope of this orthodox education, there was no place for a study of the vernacular. Writing in the early sixteenth century, the Spanish humanist, Vives, had sanctioned its use in teaching the rudiments of Latin grammar, where speed and clarity were necessary; and towards the end of the sixteenth century in England, the increasing burden of the curriculum in higher forms of the grammar school, where Greek and Hebrew were introduced, must have put pressure on the time available lower down the school for acquiring the grammatical rules. At least, the older ideal of Erasmus and Colet, of studying the grammar alongside elementary texts, subsequently seems to have given way to separate formal instruction in grammar, as a preliminary to the classical education proper. Moreover, a good grammar school could not afford to expend time in teaching the rudiments of the alphabet, and a child entering the grammar school at the age of seven or thereabouts might well be expected to have some grounding in his letters, if not in accidence. Lily's *Grammar* was reissued in an English version in 1577; and in 1582, Richard Mulcaster published *The First Part of the Elementarie*, a work designed to extend and improve preliminary instruction, by providing parents and teachers in the petty schools with a guide for instructing the child in reading and writing English, thus facilitating his further studies. Mulcaster's chief concern, however, was not for the grammar schools (though he was High Master of Merchant Taylors'), but for the English language itself.

[4] I have found much useful information in M. L. Clarke, *Classical Education in Great Britain 1500-1900*, 1959.

4

But within the grammar schools, even where English was used as a convenient medium of elementary instruction, it was not an object of study. In 1627 John Brinsley, the author of *Ludus Literarius*, knew of no school that had regard for training its scholars 'in the proprietie, puritie, and copie of our English tongue'. Brinsley wanted to see the introduction of exercises in English translation and composition, and he cited three reasons, the first two of which were familiar enough in his time, that English was the language of common usage, and that to advance its 'puritie and elegance' was further to imitate the Greeks and Romans, who did as much for their native tongues. Brinsley's third argument, however, is one that anticipates developments to come: 'Because of those which for a time are trained up in Schooles, there are very few which proceed in learning, in comparison of them that follow other callings'.[5]

In the event, the grammar schools and universities pursued a purely classical curriculum until the nineteenth century, despite Thomas Sheridan's enlightened proposal in 1763, that young gentlemen at the universities should acquire 'a grammatical knowledge of our mother tongue, and a critical skill therein, together with the art of reading it with propriety, and reciting it publicly with judgment and grace'.[6] During the seventeenth century, however, an alternative education was to become available for 'them that follow other callings'. A reaction against the study of 'words' rather than 'things' was launched in England in 1605, with Bacon's *Advancement of Learning*, the authoritative programme of reform in the name of scientific humanism:

Scholars in universities come too soon and too unripe to logic and rhetoric arts fitter for graduates than children and novices: for these two, rightly taken, are the gravest of sciences, being the arts of arts; the one for judgment, the other for ornament: and they be the rules and directions how to set forth and dispose matter; and therefore for minds empty and unfraught with matter, and which have not gathered that which Cicero calleth *Sylva* and *Supellex*, stuff and variety, to begin

---

[5] J. Brinsley, *Ludus Literarius or the Grammar Schoole* (1627), ed. E. T. Campagnac, 1917, p. 22.
[6] T. Sheridan, *A Course of Lectures on Elocution* (1763). Quoted by S. I. Tucker, *English Examined*, 1961, p. 110.

with those arts (as if one should learn to weigh, or to measure, or to paint the wind), doth work but this effect, that the wisdom of those arts, which is great and universal, is almost made contemptible, and is degenerate into childish sophistry and ridiculous affectation.[7]

Language is not to be studied as an end in itself, but as the medium of knowledge: the subject matter is of primary importance. An influential German disciple of Bacon, Wolfgang Ratke, held that everthing should be taught first in the mother tongue, where the scholar has only to think about the content, not the words. Language is 'but the instrument conveying to us things useful to be known', as Milton wrote, and indeed it was among the Puritans that Baconian ideas of educational reform were most current. In 1641, Samuel Hartlib persuaded Parliament to invite the great Moravian reformer, Comenius, to advise them in an inquiry for establishing a universal college for the advancement of science. Bacon's influence on seventeenth-century educational thinkers is obvious enough, and but for the upheavals of the Civil War and subsequent re-entrenchment of the Church in orthodox education, the conservatism of the grammar schools and universities might not have been so rigidly maintained. Nevertheless, confronted with Puritan attacks upon humanism, Anglican spokesmen constructed a defence of the literary education in terms which in years to come could be transferred from classical learning and applied to the study of English. One such apologist, writing in 1653,[8] referred to:

that *order* and *beauty* of *eloquence* which Rhetorick teacheth: By which truths have both an edge and luster set on them, doe most *adorn* them, and *enforce* to the *quickest* prevalencies on mens mindes, and the firmest impressions on their passions and affections; that so their rationall vigour may hold out to mens actions; and extend to the ethicks or *morality* of civill conversation, which is the politure of mens hearts and hands; the softner and sweetner of violent passions, and rougher manners to the candor and equity of polity and society.

[7] F. Bacon, *The Advancement of Learning* (1605), ed. G. W. Kitchin, Everyman's Library, 1954, p. 66.
[8] J. Gauden, *Hieraspites, A Defence of the Ministry and Ministers of the Church of England*, 1653, p. 399. Quoted by R. F. Jones, 'The Humanistic Defence of Learning', *Reason and Imagination*, ed. J. A. Mazzeo, 1962, pp. 71–92.

In the event, it was the religious dissenters after the Restoration who provided a more progressive kind of education, embodying the utilitarian practical ideas of earlier reformers. The enforcement in 1662 of the Act of Uniformity deprived non-conforming ministers of their livings, excluded dissenters from the universities, and made it virtually impossible for them to teach in the grammar schools. Consequently, numbers of such ministers opened schools in their homes, and after legal difficulties were relaxed by the Act of Toleration in 1689, some of these establishments were re-constituted as Dissenting Academies. These colleges flourished up and down the country, giving a general education alternative to that of the universities. An important part of their function was the preparation and training of non-conformist clergy, though many of their pupils were destined for more worldly careers: Daniel Defoe, the son of a butcher, attended Newington Green Academy between 1676 and 1681. The sons of tradesmen were joined by those of the gentry, for the Dissenting Academies were often preferred to Oxford and Cambridge, where the life was notoriously extravagant and undisciplined.

The curriculum of the early academies was not very different from that of the universities, but Classics did not long retain an exclusive importance. Modern languages, modern history, and eventually scientific subjects came to be included in the studies, alongside divinity, Latin, Greek, and Hebrew. The hymn-writer Philip Doddridge was educated at the Kibworth Academy early in the eighteenth century; Bacon's *Essays* were studied there, and exercises were set in English composition and elocution as part of the training for the duties of the dissenting ministry. In 1729 Doddridge founded an academy at Northampton as a kind of continuation of that at Kibworth, and the Northampton Academy became one of the most famous in the country. It seems in fact to have been a cradle of English studies: Doddridge was one of the first tutors to deliver his lectures in English, and two of his pupils, Andrew Kippis and John Aikin, themselves became tutors in academies where they encouraged the study of English authors for their stylistic and literary qualities. Kippis, better known as the editor of *Biographia Britannica*, was a tutor of Belles Lettres in

Hoxton Academy, and as an example of his teaching there have survived the notes of a lecture he delivered in 1770, 'An Essay on the Variety and Harmony of the English Heroick Verse'.[9] At Warrington Academy, founded in 1757, John Aikin used to illustrate his classical lectures with quotations from modern poetry, and, according to the testimony of a former pupil, his weekly reading-class was 'often the most satisfactory and improving of any in the whole week': 'After the exercises were examined he would turn to some of the finest passages of the English poets— Milton, Pope, Thomson, Young, and Akenside, and, having first read a considerable portion, he heard each of the students read in order, and pointed out their defects'.[10] Dr. Aikin's taste for literature was evidently transmitted to his daughter, who was in later years the celebrated Mrs. Barbauld.

In 1761 Aikin was succeeded as Tutor of Languages and Belles Lettres at Warrington by Joseph Priestley, and here again the thread of continuity persists, for after Doddridge's death in 1751 his academy migrated from Northampton to the nearby Daventry, in the same year that the young Priestley became a pupil there. Now remembered chiefly for his discoveries in chemistry and electricity, Joseph Priestley was something of a universal genius, achieving distinction not only as a man of science but as a linguist and as a liberal theologian. Perhaps his multiple interests tended to impinge on each other: it is recorded that he once exorcized a demon with the help of an electrical machine.[11] A man of so much energy and such diverse talents could not stay in one place for too long, and Priestley left Warrington Academy in 1767. Just before his arrival there in 1761, he had compiled one of the earliest text-books in English studies, *Rudiments of English Grammar adapted to the use of Schools*, which included extracts from the Bible, Addison, Young, Bolingbroke, Hume, Swift, Pope, and Wolsey's farewell speech from *Henry VIII*. In these new subjects, there were often no textbooks before tutors supplied their own, and in 1774 William Enfield, subsequently tutor of Belles Lettres at Warring-

[9] H. Maclachlan, *English Education under the Test Acts*, 1931, pp. 122–3, and Appendix I, p. 290, V (c).
[10] Quoted in I. Parker, *Dissenting Academies in England*, 1914, pp. 110–11.
[11] D.N.B.

ton, published another anthology of English prose and verse, whose title, *The Speaker*, suggests that it was designed for use in elocution classes. Kippis, Aikin, Priestley, and Enfield were all honoured with degrees by Scottish universities, and doubtless the teaching of Belles Lettres in the Dissenting Academies was influenced by the Scottish model, where classes in rhetoric and logic were also beginning to study English language and literature.[12]

The Dissenting Academies imparted 'useful knowledge', in contrast to the studies of the grammar schools and universities. In 1765 Priestley published *An Essay on a Course of Liberal Education for Civil and Active Life*, in the Preface to which he maintained that 'the studies of youth should tend to fit us for the business of manhood; and . . . the objects of our attention and turn of thinking in younger life should not be too remote from the destined employment of our riper years'. Where the influence of Locke's thoroughgoing utilitarianism is so clear, we may find it paradoxical that Belles Lettres should appear in the course of studies. There were obvious practical advantages in the exercises to improve spoken and written English, but how did the acquisition of literary taste equip a young man for 'civil and active life'? The answer lies deep in the social feeling of the time, in the readiness of the middle classes to ape the tastes and standards of their social superiors. The aspirations to which Addison appealed in the *Spectator*, and on behalf of which Lord Chesterfield acclaimed Dr. Johnson's Dictionary, revealed a willingness to follow dictation in matters of correct taste, and made an acquaintance with the best authors a mark of breeding in young gentlemen not destined for any of the learned professions. It was an attitude reflected in the fruitless proposals of Thomas Sheridan for reforming the curricula of the universities.[13]

These aspirations originated in the earlier period, in that process of dilution by which the Renaissance 'courtier' became the seventeenth-century 'gentleman'. As books of courtesy came to have an appeal beyond the aristocratic milieu in which they first appeared, so the importance which they placed on the cultivation of literature

[12] See Appendix I, p. 171.   [13] See p. 5 *supra*.

was conveyed to a wider and expanding stratum of society. We can follow the percolation from Castiglione and Sir Thomas Elyot to books like John Cleland's *Institution of a Young Nobleman* (1607) and Henry Peacham's *Compleat Gentleman* (1622). Both the Stuart authors recommended their readers to cultivate the literature of their own tongue, while too much classical study was considered unbecoming to a gentleman. On the other hand, Richard Brathwaite's Puritan version of the *English Gentleman* (1630) displayed less interest in the more frivolous elegancies of literature.

As the grammar schools were exclusively concerned with the ancient tongues, there arose a feeling that some provision should be made for those whose future calling in life did not require this purely classical education. I have quoted earlier the complaint which John Brinsley made in 1627 on these grounds; in 1660, Charles Hoole took up the same question in his *New Discovery of the Old Art of Teaching Schoole*. Writing of such children 'as are intended for Trades, or to be kept as drudges at home, or employed about husbandry', he observed that 'the non-improvement of childrens time after they can read English any whit well, throweth open a gap to all loose kinde of behaviour', and suggested that they would be more profitably occupied if encouraged to further their reading in English:

And in stead of the Accidents, which they do neither understand nor profit by, they may be benefitted in reading Orthodoxal Catachismes and other Books, that may instruct them in the Duties of a Christian, such as are *The Practise of Piety, The Practise of Quietnesse, The Whole Duty of Man*; and afterwards in other delightful books of English History; as, *The History of Queen Elizabeth*; or Poetry, as *Herberts Poems, Quarl's Emblems*; and by this means they will gain such a habit and delight in reading, as to make it their chief recreation, when liberty is afforded them. And their acquaintance with good books will (by Gods blessing) be a means so to sweeten their (otherwise sowr) natures, that they may live comfortably towards themselves, and amiably converse with other persons.[14]

Hoole was perhaps over-zealous, since the children he was writing

[14] C. Hoole, *A New Discovery* (1660), ed. E. T. Campagnac, 1913, Pt. I, pp. 24-27.

of were mere eight-year-olds in the petty school, but the suggestion that English literature was the poor man's Classics showed prophetic insight. In a later chapter of this book, when he came to treat of the studies of the fourth form in the grammar school, he would have had them acquire a taste for poetry, by studying and imitating English authors alongside their Latin texts:

And now it will be requisite to try what inclination your young Scholars have towards Poetry: you may therefore let them learn to compose English verses, and to inure them so to do, you should 1. let them procure some pretty delightful and honest English Poems, by perusal wherof they may become acquainted with the Harmony of English Poesie. Mr. *Hardwicks* late Translation of *Mantuan*, Mr. *Sandys* of *Ovid*, Mr. *Ogleby's* of *Virgil*, will abundantly supply them with Heroick Verses; which after they can truly and readily make, they may converse with others, that take liberty to sport it in Lyrick verses. Amongst all which, Mr. *Herberts* Poems are most worthy to be mentioned in the first place, and next to them (I conceive Mr. *Quarles divine Poems, and his divine Fansies;*) besides which, you may allow many others full of wit and elegancie; but be sure you admit of none which are stuff't with drollary or ribauldry, which are fitter to be burnt, then to be sent abroad to corrupt good manners in youth.[15]

There is no evidence to suggest that Hoole's scheme was adopted in the orthodox curricula of the grammar schools, though there may well have been other masters like Richard Busby of Westminster School, where Dryden composed some of his first English verses in translating Persius.

Nevertheless, Hoole indicates how at first the study of English was to be closely modelled on that of the Classics. When the study of Belles Lettres is advocated, throughout the eighteenth century and even in the early nineteenth century, the same tone and assumptions are adopted, whether the subject is English or classical: an understanding of polite literature and of the principles of composition is a preparation for the attainments of the scholar and the tastes of a gentleman. Thus the Scottish professor, Hugh Blair, proclaimed in his authoritative *Lectures on Rhetoric and Belles Lettres* (1783):

[15] Ibid., Pt. III, p. 158.

In the education of youth, no object has in every age appeared more important to wise men, than to tincture them early with a relish for the entertainments of taste. The transition is commonly made with ease from these to the discharge of the higher and more important duties of life. Good hopes may be entertained of those whose minds have this liberal and elegant turn. It is favourable to many virtues, whereas, to be entirely devoid of relish for eloquence, poetry, or any of the fine arts, is justly construed to be an unpromising symptom of youth; and raises suspicions of their being prone to low gratifications, or destined to drudge in the more vulgar and illiberal pursuits of life.[16]

A similar exhortation, calculated to shame the idlest schoolboy, is reported of a master at Eton in the 1840's:

If you do not take more pains, how can you ever expect to write good longs and shorts? If you do not write good longs and shorts, how can you ever be a man of taste? If you are not a man of taste, how can you ever be of use in the world?[17]

Certainly in some quarters there remained grave doubts about the efficacy of the study of the vernacular as an educational instrument, as distinct from an end in itself: could it have the same disciplinary value, the same power to train the mind, as the challenge which confronted the student of a dead language? Charles Rollin, the French author of *The Method of Teaching and Studying the Belles Lettres*, did not think so, and his book, translated into English in 1734, was of considerable influence:

I say nothing here of the rules of French poetry, as the different exercises of the classes do not allow time enough for instruction upon that head; and besides, the reading of our own poets may be dangerous to them in several respects; but especially as it requires no pains on their parts, and presents only roses without thorns, we have cause to fear, lest it should give them a distaste to their other studies, which as they are more difficult and less agreeable, so they are infinitely more useful and important.[18]

Nevertheless, for those not privileged to benefit from the social and intellectual advantages of a classical education, the study of

[16] H. Blair, *Lectures on Rhetoric and Belles Lettres*, 1811 edn., p. 4.
[17] L. Stephen, *Life of Sir Jas. Fitzjames Stephen*, 1895, p. 81.
[18] C. Rollin, *The Method of Teaching and Studying the Belles Lettres*, 1734, p. 332.

English literature, along lines corresponding to that of Greek and Latin, offered some measure of liberal and yet practical culture. Just as Charles Hoole's refractory schoolchildren were to have their 'otherwise sowr' natures sweetened by a course of English studies, so, more than a century later, the Rev. Vicesimus Knox introduced his *Elegant Extracts*, one of the earliest school anthologies of English literature, with the idea that literature was an agent for humanizing the middle ranks of society:

There is no good reason to be given why the mercantile classes, at least of the higher order, should not amuse their leisure with any pleasures of polite literature. Nothing perhaps contributes more to liberalize their minds, and prevent that narrowness which is too often the consequence of a life attached, from the earliest age, to the pursuits of lucre.[19]

We are now encountering that view of the moral power of 'culture', which is so characteristic of the nineteenth century, and which provided the motive force behind the emergence of English studies in the reformed educational schemes of the future.

Many of the attitudes and points of view illustrated and discussed in this chapter survived for years to come: some sound familiar even today. Stemming from the distinction between the classical and scientific humanism of the Renaissance, two currents of thought, at times divergent, at times flowing paradoxically parallel, began to form the pattern of English studies. First introduced as a vehicle for teaching 'things' rather than 'words', the vernacular became itself an object of study, either as a preliminary or as a lesser alternative to classical studies. As Latin lost the practical value it once had, and as its place in education, with that of Greek, became purely literary, so the study of English literature advanced, sometimes alongside the older subjects, and generally in imitation of them. Nevertheless English studies did not lose their original associations with the more practical, anti-classical attitude to education, particularly where elocution and written composition were taught. Both utilitarian and literary ideals contributed to develop the importance of English studies as part of a well-rounded general education. Gradually, in the course of the nine-

[19] *Elegant Extracts*, ed. V. Knox, 1824 edn., Preface.

teenth century, the rhetorical approach was replaced by the historical, and the notion of literary taste as a polite acquisition gave way to a sterner moral urgency, but it was to be even longer before English was accepted as an academic discipline sufficient to itself.

II

THE LONDON COLLEGES

THE spirit of reform in early nineteenth-century England found its most articulate expression in the two great movements loosely but conveniently described as Utilitarianism and Evangelicalism. Ultimately opposed to each other, as thorough-going secularism and inspired religious idealism must be, they nevertheless often converged and coincided in their immediate aims. Indeed to Élie Halévy, writing of this period, it seemed that 'the fundamental paradox of English society is precisely the partial junction and combination of these two forces theoretically so hostile'.[1] How much more ironic is it, then, that Utilitarianism and Evangelicalism, alike in their antipathy to imaginative literature, should yet bring about those educational reforms in which English studies gained a recognized and growing importance. As the empiricists stood in the line of direct descent from Bacon and Locke, so the humanitarian and liberal ideals of the Evangelicals were inherited from the democratic enthusiasms of Puritan, and later of Wesleyan, champions of popular education. The study of English language and literature reflects this dual continuity, though changes in emphasis and approach become gradually apparent. The close association between reading and writing, the rhetorical tradition of studying those writers who are 'models of style', gives way in the course of the nineteenth century to the teaching of literature as cultural history; while the attitude to Belles Lettres as a polite acquisition, a mark of social refinement, is transformed to a profounder conception of the moral power of great literature, a belief in its humanizing influence, counteracting malignant forces in a rapidly changing society.

The curious interaction of Utilitarian and Evangelical purposes

[1] É. Halévy, *England in 1815*, trans. E. I. Watkins and D. A. Barker, 2nd edn. revised, 1949, p. 585.

is nowhere better illustrated than in the early histories of the two London colleges, where Professors of English were first instituted. University College, or, as it was first called, London University, was founded in 1826, during the year following the appearance of Henry Brougham's tract, *Practical Observations on the Education of the People*, in which he had proposed the creation of several new universities. Brougham himself played a leading part in the foundation of University College, and the spirit of philosophical radicalism is clear enough in the plans for a purely secular education. The dissenters, however, threw in their lot with the free-thinkers, and the first Librarian and Secretary to the Council was E. A. Cox, a Baptist minister from Hackney Academy. Later, in 1833, the former Northampton Academy removed to London as Coward College, whence its students attended the Arts Course of the new 'university'. The teaching of scientific subjects and modern languages shows that many features of the old academies were appropriated, and the model of the Scottish universities would naturally have suggested itself since most of the early professors, as well as Brougham and Cox, were themselves Scottish graduates. But the new departure which so shocked and alarmed more conservative opinion, and which gave the college its nickname of 'the Godless Institution of Gower Street', was the idea of an education divorced from any kind of religious qualification. The 'London University' was a challenge to the Establishment in Church and State, and this challenge was soon taken up: King's College was founded as a rival institution by Anglican and Tory interests, on the principle that religion and education cannot be separated, and opened its doors in 1831, three years later than University College. The inevitable hostility between the two colleges and their jealous refusal to co-operate, in which King's College was the more adamant, was an unfortunate state of affairs that led in 1836 to the creation of the University of London. This independent, incorporeal institution was little more than an examining body, divorced altogether from teaching and existing only to confer certificates, diplomas, and degrees. A seemingly unbounded faith in examinations is one of the least attractive aspects of nineteenth-century education, and examinations began to proliferate almost from the moment in 1826 when Brougham reported that his committee on the new college curriculum had recommended that 'examinations should in every branch be introduced'.² Until the University of London was granted its charter, the course of studies in both colleges did not lead to any degree, and this is important when considering the standard of the education they offered. The average age of their students was between sixteen and eighteen; most of the boys attended after leaving school and before going either into business or on to Oxford or Cambridge. John Ruskin, for example, spent a year at King's College, then proceeded to matriculate at Oxford in 1836.

Whilst plans for University College were still under discussion, an attack on utilitarian principles in education was made in July 1826 by the Rev. H. J. Rose in a sermon preached at Cambridge, on *The Tendency of Prevalent Opinions about Knowledge*. Rose, a friend both of Wordsworth and of John Henry Newman, was also to be a leading figure in the founding of King's College, and so it is particularly interesting that he should have made this plea for the study of literature, on the grounds that 'we can make no progress to loftier knowledge except by a proportionate elevation of being'. The language is awesome, but the sentiments have since been subscribed to often enough:

It is in a deep rooted confidence and persuasion of the truth of these principles, that we would make our earnest appeal for the revival, or if that word may not be used, for an increased attention to literature alike as an engine of education, and as the pursuit of more advanced and mature years. Neglected and despised as it is in comparison with its favoured competitor, now far more does it deserve the notice bestowed on her. It is not partial in its cultivation of the intellect, but tends at once to correct the taste, to strengthen the judgement, to instruct us in the wisdom of men better and wiser than ourselves, to exercise the reasoning faculties on subjects which demand and deserve their attention, and to show them the boundaries imposed on them by Providence. It is literature which fits and prepares us best of all for the examination of those moral and intellectual truths which are not only the worthiest exercise of our reason, but most concern our future destiny; and it is

² C. New, *The Life of Henry Brougham to 1830*, 1961, p. 374.

literature alone assuredly, which leads the Young Divine into the schools of theology, qualified to benefit either himself or others.[3]

Rose quoted a paragraph from Wordsworth's *Convention of Cintra* (1809), in a similar vein: 'While Mechanic Arts, Manufactures, Agriculture, Commerce, and all those products of knowledge which are confined to gross—definite—and tangible objects, have, with the aid of Experimental Philosophy, been every day putting on more brilliant colours; the splendour of the imagination has been fading.' The inclusion of Wordsworth reminds us that the conception of literature as a humanizing power, and in particular of the poetic imagination as endowed with a profounder moral insight, a deeper truth than that comprehended by the scientific mind, characterized one aspect of Romanticism, and that such conceptions lie behind the moral earnestness of many nineteenth-century teachers of English literature.

The distinctions which divided University College and King's College so deeply were reflected in their respective approach to English studies. At University College, as one would expect, the emphasis was upon the more practical aspects, upon composition and the more 'scientific' and factual study of language; while at King's College there was at first nothing so utilitarian as a class in composition, and the reading of English literature was encouraged on moral principles similar to those adumbrated in Rose's sermon. The difference is suggested by the respective titles of the two Chairs: at University College there was the Professor of English Language and Literature, and at King's College his counterpart was known as the Professor of English Literature and History. But the contrast is not so distinct initially, since the two Chairs were first occupied in turn by the same man.

The Rev. Thomas Dale was appointed at University College in 1828, not without some controversy, for an Evangelical clergyman could scarcely have been an obvious choice in the 'Godless Institution'. Dale's appointment in fact frustrated Bentham's hopes for his own candidate, Thomas Bowring, whose extensive

---

[3] H. J. Rose, *The Tendency of Prevalent Opinions about Knowledge Considered*, 1826, p. 11.

command of languages qualified him in Bentham's view for fulfilling his duties as Professor of English in the capacity of a
'General Secretary for Foreign Correspondence'.[4] A more
intriguing possibility might have been Thomas Carlyle, who
entertained thoughts of offering himself either as Professor of
English or for the Chair of Moral Philosophy: he soon abandoned
both these notions, however. Thomas Dale remained at University College for only two years, but in 1835 he returned to academic
life as the first Professor of English Literature and History at
King's College.

Dale's inaugural lecture, delivered at University College in
October 1828, could have left no doubt that he intended to use his
position to counteract the dangerous tendencies licensed by the
secular spirit of the College. He laid down as his first principle
that 'mental culture should be connected with moral instruction,
and both enlisted in the service of Religion', though he also made
it clear that the study of English was 'expedient for a professional
education and an essential part of a general education'. His 'plan
for the critical study of the English language as adapted to young
men who have received the rudiments of a classical education'
does not differ essentially from the rhetorical studies of the old
dissenting academies and of the Scottish universities:

1. The History of the Language, comprehending a view of its origin,
formation, progress, and perfection.—I use the term perfection in a
relative sense (for absolute perfection can be predicted of no language
whatsoever); but we may assume that a language to whose stock of
words no material addition has been made for upwards of two centuries, may now be accounted *stationary*, or perfect in proportion to its
capacity.

2. The Philosophy of the Language, under which head I include the
classification and analysis of its constituent parts, or sorts of words;
their relation to, and dependence on, each other; the principles of
pronunciation and orthography; the etymologies of words; the con-
struction of sentences; the force and harmony of periods; in short, all
that relates to the genius and structure of the language.

3. The Use and Application of the Language in the various kinds of

[4] C. New, op. cit., p. 377. See also C. K. Ogden, 'Useful and Entertaining Knowledge:
the Benthamic Tradition', *Psyche*, Vol. XVIII, 1938–52, p. 132.

speaking and composition, commencing with the plain and perspicuous, and proceeding upward to the elevated and majestic style.

But when he turns to discuss the study of literature, the Evangelical clergyman supersedes the pedagogue. Reaffirming with passionate determination that 'moral and religious principles are infinitely more momentous to the character and interests of the future man' than 'mere intellectual improvement', he warms to his subject, with something of that 'elevated and majestic style' befitting a teacher of rhetoric:

In the history of our literature, more particularly of the drama, it will be my painful duty to point out too many names which exemplify this assertion—too many, whose wreath of imperishable laurel is interwoven with bitter and deadly herbs, which, like the envenomed diadem that encircled the brow of the Christian virgin in the days of fiery persecution, insinuate a subtle poison into the veins, and convey it even to the heart! . . . But in all my Lectures, more particularly when treating upon that glorious and inexhaustible subject, the LITERATURE of our country—I shall esteem it my duty—and I trust I shall find it my delight—to inculcate lessons of virtue, through the medium of the masters of our language. Nor to those parents who are acquainted with the earlier productions of English literature will such a declaration appear superfluous or misplaced. *They* know, that the gems with which it is so copiously adorned, sometimes require to be abstracted and exhibited with a careful hand, lest they should convey pollution with the foul mass of daring profaneness or disgusting wantonness in which they are too often incrusted. *They* at least, therefore, will appreciate my motive, when I declare, that never, in tracking the course of those brilliant luminaries that sparkle in the firmament of our literature—never will I suffer the eye of inexperienced youth to be dazzled by the brilliancy of genius, when its broad lustre obscures the deformity of vice; never will I affect to stifle the expression of a just indignation, when wit, taste, and talent, have been designedly prostituted by their unworthy possessors to the excitement of unholy passions, the palliation of guilty indulgences, the ridicule of virtue, or the disparagement of religion.[5]

Dale does not actually indict any authors by name here, no doubt wisely in view of that perverse inclination of youth to taste for-

[5] T. Dale, *An Introductory Lecture Delivered in the University of London*, 1828, p. 30.

bidden sweets, but it seems that when Professor Dale had cautiously sifted them, the 'gems' of English literature would no longer be quite so 'glorious and inexhaustible'. It is painful to have to record that the first Professor of English began his career with a vehement attack on literature. Nevertheless Dale's attitude is not essentially different from that of H. J. Rose; he too would have held, in the words of the sermon already mentioned, that 'it is literature which fits and prepares us best of all for the examination of those moral truths which are not only the worthiest exercise of our reason, but most concern our future destiny'. Behind the florid oratory of the inaugural lecture burns the same moral zeal that promoted English studies throughout the century.

The burden of Dale's duties at University College, however, was in language rather than literature. He lectured three times a week to a regular class on the principles of composition. During the first year there were thirty-two students following the English course, an enrolment considerably smaller than that for other classes: 102 for Latin, seventy-nine for Greek, over a hundred each in Science and Mathematics, while the largest class was that in English Law, with 144 students. Most students enrolled for more than one course, but of the 300 who entered the college in this opening session, the greater proportion were in the medical school. Dale apparently miscalculated in expecting 'the rudiments of a classical education' from all his students: many of them were of a more elementary attainment. He therefore divided the English course into senior and junior classes for the second year, when the numbers rose to twenty-four in the former and fifty-two in the latter, as the total number of students in the college almost doubled.[6]

As we have seen, a regular examination system was to be introduced in all subjects, and the first annual examination in English gives some indication of the kind of studies pursued by the regular students. To judge from the nature of the questions, the principle test was of ability to remember the Professor's prescribed answers.

[6] *University of London, Distribution of the Prizes and of the Certificates of Honour*, 1828–9, pp. 5–6; 1829–30, p. 27. This and other material relating to the early prospectuses, examinations, and annual reports, used in the present chapter, are kept in the library of University College, London.

There is not much scope for the critical imagination in such questions as these:

Who is the first distinguished writer of English prose? Point out the characteristic features of his style, and say in what respect it differs from that of Lord Clarendon.

When is the translation of an idiomatic expression perfect?

Why is D a perfect letter?

The 'Questions for students of the English class' comprised a four-hour paper drawn up in the style of a catechism. The paper had five sections: History of the English Language, Grammar of the English Language, Principles and Practice of English Composition, Translations from Classical Authors into English, and Rhetoric. Shakespeare was included for his bad grammar:

Derive and conjugate the irregular verb to break, and state whether there is any grammatical error in the following:
'I have *broke* with her father, and his good will obtained'—*Shakespeare*.

As he promised in his inaugural address, Dale also lectured on English literature, though these lectures were designed for a more general audience, and were, as the introductory outline explained, 'altogether distinct from those on the ENGLISH LANGUAGE; being not only directed to an essentially different object, but adapted indiscriminately to students of all descriptions, regular or occasional'. This 'essentially different object' was doubtless the elucidation of the moral agency of great literature, and whatever his utilitarian employers thought of it, Dale evidently regarded this aspect of his duties as no less important, for he prepared an impressive scheme of four lecture courses on literature, 'for the accommodation of gentlemen who may find it inconvenient to attend the whole'. Unfortunately only the titles of these lectures remain, and these suggest that Dale approached literature by rhetorical forms and *genres*, as did the teachers of Belles Lettres in the previous century. He advertised, amongst others, eight lectures on Dramatic Poetry, six on Epic Poetry, five on Divinity, and one on the History of Romantic Fiction—perhaps coming as close as he considered prudent to the novel, that corrupter of youthful morals. There were also some lectures on the History of English Literature, and it would be interesting to know what was contained in that auctioneer's lot he described as 'Miscellaneous Poetry of the 1st Period'.

Nothing survives to satisfy this curiosity, but between Dale's resignation from University College in 1830 and his appointment in 1835 at King's College, he opened a school in Camberwell, where one of his pupils was John Ruskin. Ruskin followed Dale to King's College for a short time, where he read Classics privately with him, and also attended some of his lectures in the college. Ruskin's remarks on his studies under Dale therefore throw some further light on Dale's qualities as a Professor of English. Ruskin does not seem to have had any great affection for his teacher, and later recorded his low estimation quite unequivocally:

The lectures were on early English literature, of which, though I had never read a word of any before Pope, I thought myself already a much better judge than Mr. Dale.[7]

In fact the young Ruskin was moved by Dale's evangelical prejudices to write for his tutor an 'Essay on Literature', in defence of Scott, Bulwer Lytton, and Byron; the essay was found among Dale's papers after his death. It is a common experience of teachers of literature to find that the tastes of their brighter pupils are somewhat more up-to-date than their own.

A letter from Ruskin to his father in March 1836 reveals a little more of Dale's approach to his subject:

My dearest Father—I sit down to write of I know not what. I intend to commence with our third lecture, English literature. Four lectures on this subject have spoken of four celebrated authors of old time—Sir John Mandevill, Sir John Gower, Chaucer, and Wickliffe. We are made acquainted with their birth, parentage, education, etc.; the character of their writings is spoken of, and extracts are read as examples of their style. These extracts are always interesting, frequently entertaining, sometimes laughable, although the laugh of the hearer is generally at, not with, the author.[8]

[7] *The Works of John Ruskin*, ed. E. T. Cook and A. Wedderburn, 39 vols., 1903, xxxv. 178.
[8] Ibid., xxxvi. 6.

It is good to know that Dale was apparently not without a sense of humour, for on the whole he cuts a stern and censorious figure in this history. By no means tolerant as a critic, his scholarship does not seem to have been altogether above suspicion. This at least is the impression given by one further piece of evidence as to his academic abilities: in 1845 he re-issued Hugh Blair's *Lectures on Rhetoric and Belles Lettres*, the last edition of a work that had had a long and influential life since its first appearance in 1783. Dale prefaced his edition with an extensive introductory essay, correcting (not always justifiably) and supplementing his original, and giving a cursory survey of English literary history. Though Dale had left King's College five years previously, there seems no reason to suppose that his views had materially changed since the days when he had expressed them in his professorial lectures, and the following unsympathetic but spirited assessment of *Beowulf* is probably not very different from that heard by his students in the London colleges:

The most complete poetical production extant in this language is the Romance of Beowulf, a kind of Saxon Iliad, which has recently been edited by an accomplished Saxon scholar,[9] and is further remarkable as being the earliest composition of an heroic kind in any vernacular language of Europe. It is characterized by the usual strain of Saxon sentiment, representing the drunken carousal as the chief of joys, and courage in the field as the first of duties, and with scarcely a recognition of the existence of a second sex. If to be poetical is to be imaginative, man is never likely to become so till he has learned to write on woman. The Saxons never learnt this, and therefore their poetry during five centuries is nearly at par, and would have continued so until the present hour had they confined themselves to the congenial themes of the 'play of swords' (*gaudia certaminis*), or the joys of the bowl. The reason of this may be sought in nature; they who delight in bloodshed will ever be the few, and they who degrade intelligence by intoxication will rarely be the many; and verses only of universal interest can command universal attention—'Love rules the court, the camp, the grove,' and where is love without woman, and what is poetry without love?[10]

[9] The first scholarly edition of *Beowulf* was edited by J. M. Kemble in 1833, and in two volumes with a translation in 1835–7.
[10] H. Blair, *Lectures on Rhetoric and Belles Lettres*, ed. T. Dale, 1845, p. xxii.

I have dwelt at some length on the Rev. Thomas Dale, not only because he deserves commemoration as the first Professor of English, but also because his comparatively brief academic career does illustrate the main features of the study of English language and literature in the first half of the nineteenth century. At University College, Dale had been succeeded in 1830 by Alexander Blair, who preserved the dual arrangement of a junior and senior class, but abolished the annual examination and presentation of certificates, offering instead an essay prize in the junior class. The latter was instructed in the principles of English grammar, and in the rudiments of Rhetoric, while the senior class was occupied with the principles of general grammar (known to Joseph Priestley at Warrington Academy as universal grammar), and with the study of Anglo-Saxon. In his Annual Report for 1833, Blair also spoke of the senior class 'reading our greater poets in succession from Chaucer to the present day'. But studies in language and composition were very much to the fore, and when in 1836 Blair was succeeded by Henry Rogers, a Congregational minister, the annual examination was restored, and in so far as the surviving question papers indicate the substance of the course, they show that rhetoric and the qualities of style were the basis of instruction. In 1839 Robert Gordon Latham came to the Chair: his work as a philologist, a student of the existing processes in language rather than of the historical philology of the German school, has recently been aptly recalled and reappraised by Professor Quirk in his inaugural lecture as a successor in the same college.[11] Latham was a man of many interests, and later gained public distinction in medicine and in ethnology, to match the private notoriety of his eccentric personality.[12] While at University College, Latham taught Elizabethan drama and seventeenth-century poetry, as well as Anglo-Saxon, though some of the examination questions he set suggest a rather forbidding emphasis on fact:

Give reasons for believing Deckar [*sic*] *not* to have been the Crispinus of Ben Jonson's *Poetaster*.

[11] R. Quirk, *The Study of the Mother Tongue*, 1961.
[12] An amusing episode involving Latham is recounted in H. Hale Bellot, *University College, London, 1826–1926*, 1929, p. 114.

State what you know concerning the *personal* history of Donne, Cowley, Lee, Butler, and Otway.

Name the poems, first, of Addison, second, of Mallet, that have been attributed to Marvell.

After Latham, in 1845, Tom Taylor became Professor of English, though he does not appear to have allowed his interests as a fashionable dramatist to interfere with his academic duties. His examination papers on English language and literature up to Chaucer were composed entirely of questions on philology and translation: they no doubt reflect the bias of his lectures.

But when A. J. Scott succeeded Taylor in 1848, he made his inaugural lecture a plea for a more liberal study of literature:

I cannot flatter myself that there is a recognition in the public mind of the propriety of making the literature of England enter into the academic course, at all corresponding with that which the language has attained for itself.

For the first time, the historical approach to literature, as distinct from the rhetorical approach or from facts about literary history, was adumbrated as the proper method of study. 'A poet of the first order is the voice of a great era,' Scott averred. Literature was to be related to society, and studied as the expression of the culture of an age:

It only remains to subjoin, that a vernacular literature is that of a speech and of a nation both yet living, and in whose life he partakes who is to study them; and we shall have completed our description—for as a definition it is not offered—of that whose place and function in the academical course is now in question. It is the utterance of the free action of mind in its wholeness or concrete existence, under the conditions of the character and circumstance of our own people.[13]

The study of historical 'background' was allotted an important place in Scott's courses, and the following examination question, set during his brief tenure of the Chair, indicates the new direction now followed by English studies:

Mention the events and circumstances having most influence on the literary character of Elizabeth's age.

[13] A. J. Scott, *On the Academical Study of a Vernacular Literature*, 1848, pp. 4–11.

In 1850 Scott left University College to become the first Principal of Owens College, Manchester, and his place was taken for a short while by that inheritor of unfulfilled renown, Arthur Hugh Clough. David Masson succeeded to the Chair in 1852, and with the author-to-be of the voluminous *Life of Milton*, the historical study of English literature was firmly established in University College.

When King's College was opened in 1831, it had been decided that the Department of General Literature and Science should include three Professors, in Mathematics, in Classics, and in English Literature and History. But though the first two Chairs were filled, that of English Literature and History was at first left vacant, probably for lack of money. To supply the deficiency in teaching, however, the Professor of Mathematics gave some instruction in history, and the Professor of Classics gave weekly readings from edifying authors. In the first year there were sixty-four students following the general course, but thereafter the numbers rose to maintain an average intake of one hundred students until the middle of the century. In 1835, as we have seen, Dale became the first Professor of English Literature and History, after Robert Southey had declined an invitation to hold the post. Dale's retirement from academic life in 1840 brought to the Chair F. D. Maurice. He taught English history up to the Reformation, and in English literature prescribed a detailed study of the General Prologue to the *Canterbury Tales*, a text beloved of examiners since. Maurice's lectures are reported to have been somewhat abstract, with a marked avoidance of facts, and far above the heads of his students. Nevertheless, Maurice is an important figure in the development of English studies, though his contribution was made not so much in formal education, but in what we should now term 'extra-mural work'. The nature of his importance is therefore left for discussion in the next chapter.[14]

During the first half of the nineteenth century, then, English studies had changed considerably in the London colleges—and in this period they were scarcely taught anywhere else in England.

[14] F. J. C. Hearnshaw, *A Centenary History of King's College, London*, 1929, pp. 88–89, 156–7.

The contrasted social and educational views which characterized University College and King's College from their respective origins, are reflected in the progress made by each of them in furthering the study of English. In University College, the old rhetorical traditions eventually lost their hold, as the study of grammar receded before the coming of philology and Anglo-Saxon, and the study of literary *genres* became gradually orientated in literary history. Here, under the succession of Professors after Dale, English studies retained a certain astringency, never straying far from hard facts, and firmly disciplined by an examination system. If it is not too fanciful to see in these traits the legacy of Utilitarian empiricism, then in the lofty moral tone of English studies at King's College, from the ideals of Rose's sermon through the dedicated zeal of Dale and Maurice, there flows that missionary spirit which I have associated with Evangelicalism, and which did even more to promote the study of English literature outside the colleges. These two traditions cannot be kept wholly distinct from each other, but if it is an exaggeration to say that the first shaped and regularized English studies as an academic discipline while the second broadened their appeal and gave them a purpose and relevance, then this is the exaggeration of an important difference.

III

AN EDUCATION FOR THE INDUSTRIAL CLASSES

THE history of formal education is not a thing *per se* which stands alone; underlying important developments in the academic world there are always complex changes in society itself. I have tried to show how the promotion of English studies in the two London colleges was the result of a complex interaction between the spirits of Utilitarianism and Evangelicalism; but when we turn from schools and universities to more informal kinds of education, the flux and pressure of social conditions impinge even further upon our attention. The nineteenth century was a great age of educational expansion, in which the various threads of development are not easily detached from that vast web of social, economic, and intellectual change called the Industrial Revolution. The fact remains that during this time an increasing proportion of the population became literate, and that from certain influential quarters they were encouraged to read English literature of the past, as well as, sometimes as an antidote for, the more ephemeral and perhaps corrupting reading-matter of their own time. There are historians who regard the Industrial Revolution as a misleading term for processes that were operating as early as the sixteenth century, but certainly these processes accelerated rapidly towards the end of the eighteenth century, and, what is equally important, those living in the early nineteenth century were themselves acutely aware of far-reaching changes affecting a traditional stability in English society.

The spread of literacy was not dependent on the regular forms of education, but was fostered mainly by a combination of philanthropy and self-help. What distinguishes the movement for popular education is its concern, not with children, but with adults. Many children of the humbler classes had been taught their letters, and some useful employment, in the charity schools and dames' schools of the eighteenth century, though how long they subsequently maintained their precarious grasp on literacy is open to question. The ability to read and write without difficulty requires regular practice, and the nature of their lives rendered literacy a superfluous attainment for many of these children. A new departure, however, is marked by the spread of Sunday-schools for all ages, after Robert Raikes opened his school in Gloucester in 1780, and by the Adult School movement which began at the turn of the century. There must have been a genuine demand for literacy in those men who sought instruction after the long and arduous working-hours then common. And here again we find that the religious and utilitarian attitudes converged in furthering universal literacy.

On the one hand was the Protestant emphasis on the private conscience, which placed special importance upon the ability to read the Bible for oneself. Many of the Christian philanthropists, indeed, had confined their educational energies to this sole end, and could not be persuaded that there was any necessity to teach writing as well. Perhaps, too, at one time, utilitarian reason was on their side: literacy is not an end in itself. Matthew Arnold's observation, that 'No man, who knows nothing else, knows even his Bible', would have seemed rank heresy to these early zealots, if indeed the remark was altogether a truism when it was written in 1869.[1] The Methodist Revival, however, was more liberal in fostering popular reading tastes, without descending to secularism. Charles Wesley published popular editions of the more edifying and pious classics of English literature, and enabled his followers to supplement their Bibles with Bunyan and Milton. *The Pilgrim's Progress* (1743) was followed in 1763 by *An Extract from 'Paradise Lost' with Notes*; Wesley adapted the epic poem for unlearned readers by removing some 2,000 lines of the more abstruse classical references, supplying brief explanations of the difficult words, and marking with asterisks those passages which he thought 'peculiarly excellent' and recommended for memorizing.[2]

---

[1] M. Arnold, *Culture and Anarchy* (1869), ed. J. Dover Wilson, 1932, p. 154.
[2] O. Sherwin, 'Milton for the Masses', *Modern Language Quarterly*, XII, 1951, p. 269.

In his desire to bring sweetness and light to those whose lives were brutalized or spiritually impoverished by the economic conditions of society, Wesley was a forerunner of many later missionaries of culture in industrial England. The attitude became secularized, even to the point where Arnold could foresee literature as a substitute for religion, but in its essence the notion persisted that somehow literature could be used as a humanizing agency to counteract the soul-destroying evils of a rapidly changing society. To the Evangelical Knox, in a passage I have already cited, it seemed that the 'mercantile classes' would derive most benefit from 'polite literature', which would 'liberalize their minds, and prevent that narrowness which is too often a consequence of . . . the pursuits of lucre'. Similar sentiments could be attributed to teachers of literature throughout the century, except that the mercantile classes are replaced as objects of welfare by the industrial artisans, and instead of the pursuits of lucre, the corrupting influences become the oppressive conditions in mines and factories and cities, and the dangerous political extremism that was bred there.

On the other hand the spread of literacy, and the beginnings of adult education, were also prompted by more practical considerations. What Joseph Priestley had written for the middle classes was becoming equally true for their social inferiors: 'the situation of things is vastly different from what it was two or three centuries ago . . . the objects of human attention are prodigiously multiplied'.[3] One aspect of the social and economic changes was the increased complexity of life, in which the new social relationships, and the new scientific principles affecting the daily lives of more and more people, depended on the printed word. Literacy became necessary in order to understand all but the most immediate facts of existence.

This utilitarian approach to adult education was embodied in the foundation of the Mechanics' Institutes. Beginning with the London Mechanics' Institute, founded in 1823 with Brougham's influential support, similar institutes were soon established all over the country, especially in the industrial areas. There were twenty

[3] J. Priestley, *An Essay on a Course of Liberal Education* (1765), 2nd edn., 1768, p. 4.

in existence by the end of 1824, and another seventy came into being during the following year: by 1850, there were over 500 of them.[4] The original purpose of the Mechanics' Institutes was to give working men an understanding of the scientific principles underlying their new mechanical trades. But from the beginning the appetite for useful knowledge, and for self-improvement, took other forms as well. Much to the alarm of those observers who feared the popularity of Tom Paine's ideas and the spread of democratic revolution after the Napoleonic Wars, there was a persistent demand for classes in 'political economy', while scientific instruction often languished because the mechanics lacked the necessary elementary education to enable them to benefit from anything more advanced. Thus the institutes were regarded by some as hotbeds of sedition, while others thought that giving education to working men was the only way of averting revolution. And in this respect, the Mechanics' Institutes played an important part in the development of English studies, for most of them included lectures on English literature in their programmes, and through their libraries they enabled many members to develop the reading habit and to make some acquaintance with the national literature.

In their subsequent history, the character of these institutions varied from one place to another. Some failed to attract manual workers, and became more generally 'cultural', sometimes offering little more than entertainment. Some on the other hand were important and serious centres of adult education, eventually, as at Nottingham and Leicester, handing on the torch to new 'civic' universities. The London Mechanics' Institute itself was renamed Birkbeck College, after the man who had first inspired the movement, and was incorporated in London University in the 1870's. 'They have established the right of the people to culture', wrote James Hole in *The History and Management of Literary, Scientific, and Mechanics' Institutions*, an essay which won the Prize of the Society of Arts in 1853. But Hole was severely critical of their dilettante tendencies, and deplored their failure to provide a systematic education. 'The action of our Institutes', he com-

[4] C. New, *The Life of Henry Brougham to 1830*, 1961, p. 339.

plained, 'has been all in the direction of *reading*, while *study* has had to take care of itself.' He regarded with suspicion the popularity of their libraries, and remarked rather sourly on 'the small demand for instructive works as compared with those whose principal aim is amusement'. His statistics, from a sample of forty-three institutes, show that while the number of scientific lectures had dwindled since the 1830's to a third of the total lectures, those on literature had increased to more than half of the total. And he observed with some justice of these literature lectures that though 'highly valuable as an intellectual pastime for a leisure hour, the positive acquisitions can be but small'.[5] Among the most popular lecturers who visited these institutes were Charles Dickens, Cowden Clarke, and Charles and Fanny Kemble with their Shakespearian readings. Literature was not treated very academically in the Mechanics' Institutes, but surely it is not altogether a matter for regret that the artisans managed to resist those, whether of utilitarian or evangelical turn of mind, who tried to instil the notion that reading literature was a profitable study, a means of self-improvement, and forgot its appeal first and foremost as a pleasure and amusement.

A characteristic example of this untrained but real enthusiasm for the 'classics' occurs in the Chartist Thomas Cooper. Cooper, like other serious-minded artisans, was a self-educated man, and after the days of Chartism, he made several tours to lecture in these institutes, on literary topics as well as on politics. In his autobiography he recounted his youthful discovery of English literature:

Blair's 'Lectures on Rhetoric and Belles Lettres' was another book that I analysed very closely and laboriously, being determined on acquiring a thorough judgment of style and literary excellence. All this practice seemed to destroy the desire of composing poetry of my own. Milton's verse seemed to overawe me, as I committed it to memory, and repeated it daily; and the perfection of his music, as well as the gigantic stature of his intellect, were fully perceived by my mind. The wondrous knowledge of the heart unfolded by Shakespeare, made me

[5] J. Hole, *An Essay on the History and Management of Literary, Scientific, and Mechanics' Institutions*, 1853, pp. 27–32.

33

shrink into insignificance; while the sweetness, the marvellous power of expression and grandeur of his poetry seemed to transport me, at times, out of the vulgar world of circumstances in which I lived bodily.[6]

Much of the teaching of English literature in adult education was teaching by inspiration, concerned merely to encourage the reading of great authors of the past. Perhaps it still is, often enough. But if to describe this as the study of English literature is to make too high a claim for it, it is nevertheless an important part of the development of English studies. For the popularity of these informal lectures on literature, from the Mechanics' Institutes to the university extension classes, eventually impinged directly on the movement to establish English studies in the curricula of the two ancient universities.

James Hole conceded in his Essay that lectures on literature to mechanics would make them less open to corruption by the abundance of cheap sensational fiction then coming into circulation. Charles Knight, the publisher to Brougham's Society for the Diffusion of Useful Knowledge, was also anxious about the poisonous effects of 'railway fiction'.[7] Like William and Robert Chambers earlier in the century, and John Cassell a little later, he used his press to help the newly-literate classes to educate themselves, and his *Penny Cyclopaedia* came out in weekly numbers between 1833 and 1844. In the 1840's and 1850's Knight brought out nearly a dozen different editions of Shakespeare. The trade in reprints of 'classical' English literature had begun towards the end of the previous century, when John Bell, John Cooke, and John Harrison enterprisingly published the poets, dramatists, essayists, and novelists in cheap numbers. Bell's *Shakespeare* appeared in 1774, his *Poets of Great Britain Complete from Chaucer to Churchill* in 109 volumes at 1s. 6d. each from 1776 (comprehensive, if not actually 'complete'), and his *British Theatre* in twenty-one volumes at 6d. each in the same year. John Harrison's *Novelist's Magazine* began in 1780, while Cooke's sixpenny weekly numbers were the boyhood reading of Leigh Hunt, Hazlitt, and John Clare. In the 1820's, Whittingham, Limbrid,

---

[6] T. Cooper, *Life of Thomas Cooper, Written by Himself*, 1872, p. 63.
[7] See his *The Old Printer and the Modern Press*, 1854.

Sharpe, and Dove undertook more such reprints, of which one of the best-remembered, the *Aldine Edition of British Poets*, was first brought out by William Pickering in 1829, at 5s. a volume. The coming of the steam-driven press and machine-made paper in the 'thirties and 'forties, with the increasing demand for reading-matter, lowered printing costs, and in 1861 the paper duty was finally repealed. In the second half of the century, *Chandos Classics* sold 3,500,000 volumes between 1868 and 1884, and a quarter of a million of *Kent's Miniature Library of the Poets* were bought in five years; *Blackwood's Universal Library of Standard Authors* (1872) and *Moxon's Popular Poets* (1879) are only another two of the more familiar among a proliferation of uniform editions and series of English classics.[8] The student of English literature would not have found his material hard to come by, though the production of textbooks specially annotated for schools and for examination purposes is a different aspect of the subject which I shall leave for the next chapter.

A venture in adult education rather different from that of the Mechanics' Institutes was the Working Men's College. Growing from evening classes and lectures given by a group of philan-thropical professors from King's College in 1852 (when F. D. Maurice lectured on 'The Historical Plays of Shakespeare'), the college was officially opened in 1854. Although Maurice became the first Principal and his spirit pervaded the college, the initial inspiration was derived from a similar experiment in adult education, begun in the north of England twelve years before.[9] The People's College in Sheffield was founded in 1842 by a non-conformist minister, Robert Slater Bayley; he believed that the object of popular education was the acquisition of 'sound moral and mental habits', more immediately to combat the dangerous doctrines of Chartism. This kind of philanthropy appealed to the Christian Socialists: it was an idealism after their own hearts. But they also admired the self-supporting and mutually-assisting basis of the People's College, and it served as their model in planning the Working Men's College. In an essay recollecting Maurice's

[8] R. D. Altick, *The English Common Reader*, Chicago, 1957, pp. 53–59, 235–73.
[9] G. C. Moore Smith, *The Story of the People's College, Sheffield, 1842–78*, 1912.

part in founding the college, his surviving colleague J. Llewelyn Davies later tabled the four principles underlying the institution:

1. That every man was a spiritual being, whether he knew it or not. Order and relation were more important than equality.
2. All institutions and history had a Divine purpose. Civilisation meant being more civil: the raising of human fellowship to a higher level and power.
3. No rigid code of the Church was necessary: colleagues, whether atheists or dissenters, showed a true Christian spirit in service.
4. The idea of a 'college' was that of a little society, a fellowship of teachers and learners.[10]

This is a spirit in radical contrast to the practical utilitarian motives which led to the establishment of the Mechanics' Institutes. When in 1853 Maurice was dismissed from King's College, for refusing to believe in eternal damnation, he was at liberty to devote himself to popular education. His lectures show that he tried to bring out of literature the same moral and quasi-religious principles that were embodied in the practical life of the Working Men's College. Literature offered contact with great minds, and a bond of fellowship between men regardless of class or epoch. This is a special extension of Romanticism in the direction of Christian Socialism, and Maurice refers to the poet in terms that recall Wordsworth and Shelley: 'He is not, then, a more special man than we are; he is more of a common man. The human sympathies have been more awakened in him than in us.'[11] Addressing the college in 1863, Maurice evaluated two kinds of knowledge, the factual and the spiritual, in the distinction between 'acquisition' and 'illumination'.[12] He would have subscribed to the view expressed by H. J. Rose in his sermon some forty years previously, that 'we can make no progress to loftier knowledge except by a proportionate elevation of being'. As a teacher of literature, in fact, Maurice illustrates the continuity of the evangelical belief in the humanizing moral power of literature.

[10] *The Working Men's College, 1854–1904*, ed. J. Llewelyn Davies, 1904, 'F. D. Maurice', pp. 8–10.
[11] F. D. Maurice, *The Friendship of Books and Other Lectures*, ed. T. Hughes, 1874, 'Edmund Burke', p. 314.
[12] Ibid., 'Acquisition and Illumination', p. 339.

Unlike Thomas Dale, however, he made no attempt at judicial criticism, his main endeavour being simply to arouse the enthusiasm of these working men for great literature, and he therefore preferred

> that best of kind of criticism which delights to draw forth the sense and beauty of a book, and is able to do so because the heart of the critic is in sympathy with the heart of the writer.[13]

Since very little bad literature finds its way into academic syllabuses, this adaptation of the romantic spirit becomes a sensible pragmatic approach to the subject. The teaching of literature is inseparable from the teaching of criticism, surely, but while we have to deal with the literature of six centuries or more, limited sympathies are at the least a severe handicap.

Maurice was impatient of anything that came between the reader and the author, and placed little value on details of scholarship. Lecturing on *Paradise Lost*,[14] he advised his audience:

> Read it thus, and you will need no critics to tell you about its sublimity, or to classify it with books to which it has probably very little resemblance. It will come to you with its own evidence and power, as the voice of a man, but a voice which can make the deepest mind of a grand age of English history intelligible to our age; a voice which can teach us how all ages are united in Him who is, and was, and is to come. That seems to me the way of reading 'Paradise Lost'; and therefore it is that I said that the passages which exhibit to us the poet's personal sorrows and consolations are no episodes in it, but give us the key to its inmost meaning.

What Maurice thought of F. J. Furnivall, his colleague in the Working Men's College, has not come down to us, apart from the conflicts over Furnivall's secular Sundays, when he took the students for long country rambles. Furnivall taught English grammar in the college, and lectured on poetry from Chaucer to Tennyson. He was not a Christian, and had been a student at University College before matriculating at Cambridge in 1842. His approach to literature was very different from that of Maurice, and much of his rather athletic energy was expended in treating

[13] Ibid., 'On Critics', p. 388.   [14] Ibid., 'Milton', p. 266.

those *minutiae* of fact for which Maurice had little time. Industri-ously editing and publishing medieval Arthurian romances, in 1864 he was prominent in the foundation of the Early English Texts Society. He had a positive genius for founding societies, in fact, and these activities must have taken much of his attention from his teaching duties. In 1868, at the suggestion of Henry Bradshaw, he founded the Chaucer Society, followed by the Ballad Society. He went on to establish the New Shakspere Society (he was adamant about the spelling) in 1873, 'to determine the succession of his plays'. This project, on the German model, laid stress on metrical tests, and provoked the ridicule of Swin-burne, whose aesthetic sensibilities were outraged by the applica-tion of statistics to poetry. His satire on 'The Newest Shakespeare Society' appeared in the *Examiner* for April 1876, but Furnivall gave as good as he received, referring to his antagonist as 'Pigs-brook', and there followed an acrimonious 'flyting' which scarcely added to the dignity of either party.

The Working Men's College was not the only educational enterprise set on foot by Maurice: it was the second. As Tenny-son's *Princess* (1847) reminds us, a lively issue of the day was the question of education for women, and in 1848 Maurice and a few colleagues from King's College championed the cause and founded the Queen's College for Women. English literature has always been regarded, for good or evil, as a subject peculiarly fitted for the education of women, and as that movement gathered force in the second half of the century, so English studies were carried with it to the very doors of the ancient universities. How interesting, therefore, to find Charles Kingsley, in his introductory lecture as Professor of English at Queen's College, explaining (perhaps a little too rapturously) how the study of English literature would equip women for their special rôle in life:

Such a course of history would quicken women's inborn *personal interest* in the actors of this life-drama, and be quickened by it in return, as indeed it ought: for it is thus that God intended woman to look instinctively at the world. Would to God that she would teach us men to look at it thus likewise. Would to God that she would in these days claim and fulfil to the uttermost her vocation as the priestess of charity!

—that woman's heart would help deliver man from bondage to his own tyrannous and all-too-exclusive brain—from our idolatry of mere dead laws and printed books—from our daily sin of looking at men, not as our struggling and suffering brothers, but as mere symbols of certain formulae, incarnations of sets of opinions, wheels in some iron liberty-grinding or Christianity-spinning machine, which we miscall society, or civilisation, or, worst misnomer of all, the Church![15]

It is doubtful whether many of the women who since Kingsley's time have become distinguished scholars of English literature made their mark chiefly as priestesses of charity; nevertheless English studies were greatly influenced by the less utilitarian, but not for that reason less academic, spirit of women's education.

In that introductory lecture, Kingsley spoke of literature as 'the autobiography of a nation', and Maurice similarly expressed the view that 'we cannot safely separate our literary pursuits, even our literary recreations, from the history and life of our nation'.[16] The main emphasis in this moral, evangelical approach to literature is upon reading, upon the value of making contact with the great imaginations of the past; the old rhetorical connection of reading with writing had almost disappeared by the middle of the century. When the Romantics invested literature with a particular kind of authority, as a criticism and corrective of scientific rationalism, they consequently tended to isolate its function as a culture of the feelings; the attitude is typified in John Stuart Mill's tribute to the healing powers of Wordsworth's poetry, after the mental crisis of his early maturity, an episode of his *Autobiography* which is so central to an understanding of the nineteenth century. This attitude is closely related to the idea of literature as 'culture' in a wider sense: the literature of the past is called in to redress the balance of the present. However inadequately it was articulated, there was a widespread feeling that the spiritual and physical conditions of the industrial revolution impoverished the cultural lives of a large class of people, that they had been cut off from their traditional past, and that therefore they needed to be given new means of establishing connections with a national cultural

---

[15] C. Kingsley, *Works*, 28 vols., 1880–85, Vol. XX, 'On English Literature', pp. 245–65.
[16] F. D. Maurice, op. cit., 'Edmund Burke', p. 304.

heritage. Thus it was the historical approach to literature which eventually emerged, and the missionaries of adult education were particularly concerned with the industrial classes. But within formal education, too, a belief in the educational value of English literature, independent of studies in language or composition, was rapidly gaining ground. In that same year of revolutions, when Queen's College was founded, and when Kingsley pronounced literature to be the autobiography of a nation, A. J. Scott entered his plea in University College for the historical approach to English literature. When, some years before, Coleridge had envisaged the rôle of his National Church, 'at the fountainhead of the humanities, to preserve the stores and to guard the treasures of past civilization, and thus to bind the present with the past',[17] he formulated an idea which was to give impetus and shaping spirit to English studies, both as part of a general education, and as an academic discipline on its own merits.

[17] Quoted in R. Williams, *Culture and Society 1780–1950*, 1958, p. 64. This book is an extensive discussion of the complex ideas about culture as they developed during the period.

IV

THE MUSE IN CHAINS

It was not of course left to the nineteenth century to discover that literature serves a moral purpose, though Romantic critical theories, being psychological rather than rhetorical, redefined the relations between literature and life by promoting literature to the level of life. Poetry was not only about experience, it was experience itself: so, for example, Wordsworth in *The Prelude* hoped that his poetry would have 'a Power like one of Nature's'.[1] When the Romantics discussed the moral function of literature, it was not the subject matter which engaged them, as often as the intrinsic nature of poetry, and the way it operated on the imagination. Shelley's famous simile, that 'Poetry strengthens the faculty which is the organ of the moral nature of man, in the same manner as exercise strengthens a limb',[2] illustrates this new approach to literature, which lent itself readily to the psychological theories of education current in the nineteenth century. When education meant mind-training, and the subjects of the curriculum were 'instruments' to this end, literature had an obvious rôle as a culture of the feelings. Language, according to the same theory, had a similar but more astringent disciplinary value. Which literature and which language were in this respect secondary considerations, and seemed to depend on the accidents of tradition and social privilege. So Thomas Arnold observed, 'The study of language seems to me as if it was given for the very purpose of forming the human mind in youth; and the Greek and Latin languages ... seem the very instruments by which this is to be effected'.[3]

In the last chapter I tried to show why the study of English

[1] *Wordsworth's Prelude*, ed. E. de Selincourt (2nd edn. revised by H. Darbishire), 1959, Book XII (1805 version), l.312. The whole of the preceding passage, beginning at l.298, is relevant.
[2] *Shelley's Literary and Philosophical Criticism*, ed. J. Shawcross, 1909, p. 131.
[3] M. L. Clarke, *Classical Education in Britain 1500–1900*, 1959, p. 79.

literature was fostered by those most concerned with the social and moral evils of the Industrial Revolution, and how there arose an awareness of the cultural heritage embodied in the national literature. Literature was affiliated to the historical sense, and this attitude was reflected in the study of classical literature too. Dean Stanley, who was well qualified to judge, called Dr. Arnold 'the first Englishman who drew attention in the public schools to the historical, political, and philosophical value of philology and of the ancient writers, as distinguished from the mere verbal criticism and elegant scholarship of the last century'. Surprising though it is in one sense to find a common bond between the very different cultural atmospheres of adult education and the public schools, nevertheless behind both Dr. Arnold's reform of classical studies and the ideals of missionaries of culture for the industrial classes, there lay the revolution in historiography associated in particular with the new German school. Towards the end of the eighteenth century, historians became aware, not merely of states and empires, but of civilizations and cultures. Voltaire illustrated his age's consciousness of its own climactic position in the development of European culture from 'medieval barbarism', while the study of antiquity began to draw upon hitherto disregarded sources, and with such scholars as Winckelmann, Wolf, Niebuhr, and Otfried Muller, the discoveries of archaeology, the evidences of the plastic arts and of literary traditions, stimulated a new approach to the life of the past.[4] Hence in turn arose the new German school of philology, which soon revived and dominated the study of early English literature. This new historical and organic awareness of society was the immediate condition alike of a revivified approach to classical studies and of a social philosophy such as Coleridge's, 'to bind the present with the past'.

In the traditional orthodox forms of education, therefore, enthusiasm for classical literature, particularly the Greek, paralleled the moral and 'cultural' status of English literature in the rise of a new industrial democracy. It was said of John Young, Professor of Greek at Glasgow University from 1774 to 1821, that 'nothing could be more captivating than the eloquence with which he

[4] G. P. Gooch, *History and Historians in the Nineteenth Century*, 1913, pp. 1–41.

treated of the liberty, the literature and the glory of ancient Greece, while tears of enthusiasm rolled down his cheek'. No less spirited was his opposite number in Edinburgh, Andrew Dalzel; according to his former pupil Lord Cockburn, 'he inspired us with a vague but sincere ambition of literature, and with delicious dreams of virtue and poetry'.[5] Classics was given a new lease of life as a cultural education, and when in 1864 the Clarendon Commission reported on the nine public schools, they endorsed the continued supremacy of Latin and Greek with the view that there should be 'some one principal branch of study, invested with a recognized, and, if possible, a traditional importance, to which the principal weight should be assigned'. Indeed, when Dr. Kennedy of Shrewsbury School was asked by the commissioners if he were satisfied with his pupils' knowledge of English literature, he replied that he had not the time to give to the subject, and that to teach English would fritter away his power.[6] Not all the headmasters were so minded, however, and there were some like Arnold who believed firmly in the value of English essay-writing, and set passages of English poetry for exercises in translation. Some of the old classical grammar schools had in fact enlarged their curricula, and at Christ's Hospital in 1790 Coleridge had found in James Boyer a master who encouraged him to study English literature: 'he made us read Shakespeare and Milton as lessons; and they were the lessons, too, which required most time and trouble to *bring up*, so as to escape his censure'.[7] But the direct study of English in these schools is really of secondary importance to their approach to Classics, since the philosophy of a classical education was now evolving in such a way that it could be applied equally well to English studies, social traditions and mere prejudice apart.

When the Schools Enquiry Commission, otherwise known as the Taunton Commission, published their report in 1868, they revealed that nearly half of the endowed grammar schools were no longer teaching any Latin or Greek, and they endorsed the

[5] M. L. Clarke, op. cit., p. 144.
[6] *Report of the Public School Commission*, 1864, Vol. IV, Q. 470.
[7] S. T. Coleridge, *Biographia Literaria* (1817), ed. G. Watson, Everyman's Library, 1956, p. 3.

suggestion of the Rev. G. G. Bradley, Headmaster of Marl-borough School, that modern subjects should be fostered in schools of a lower social status. In a letter to the Commission, Bradley had suggested that in such schools

above all I would give unusual weight to the teaching of the English language, literature, and history, to the attempt to humanize and refine a boy's mind by trying early to familiarize him with English poetry, and to inspire him with a taste for the best authors whom I could place before him. A school which should succeed to any large extent in doing this might afford to omit from its curriculum many branches of know-ledge which are in themselves desirable.[8]

Such recommendations were echoed by an essay on 'The Teach-ing of English' which appeared in 1867, in a collection of *Essays on a Liberal Education* edited by F. W. Farrar (better remembered as the author of *Eric, or Little by Little*). The essay was contributed by J. W. Hales, who in that same year became Professor of Eng-lish at Bedford College for Women (founded in 1849), a post he was to hold for twenty-three years. Hales attacked the entrench-ment of Classics in schools, while 'English is an unknown tongue in England', and argued in terms reminiscent of those used by Joseph Priestley a century before him:

You divorce peremptorily his studies and his daily life, so that he cannot discern any sign of association between them. ... In schools whose pupils are not destined to proceed from there to a University, or to a life of studious leisure and opportunity, English should, I think, be made the prominent linguistic and literary study.[9]

Hales was seeking to dislodge Classics from their position at the centre of orthodox education, a position which he thought Eng-lish should now occupy. This concept of 'a principal branch of study', in the words of the Clarendon Report, of a subject which would serve not as a specialist training but as the centre-piece of a general education, was the ground on which Classics and English studies were henceforth to confront each other in the prolonged controversy that is still far from extinct today.

[8] *Report of the Schools Enquiry Commission*, 1868, Vol. IV, p. 420.
[9] J. W. Hales, 'The Teaching of English', *Essays on a Liberal Education*, ed. F. W. Farrar, 1867, pp. 293–310.

In 1861 the Newcastle Commission on the state of popular education had recommended that student teachers should study English language and literature 'just as the Greek and Latin Classics are read in superior public schools'.[10] Here, too, the official conclusions were closely anticipated by proposals published elsewhere: in October 1860 the newly-founded *Macmillan's Magazine* printed an article 'On the Use of English Classical Literature in the Work of Education', by the Rev. H. G. Robinson, a training-college teacher. Like Hales, Robinson attacked the dominance of classical studies, and argued that a study of English grammar, instead of Latin or Greek, was no less exacting as a discipline, and yet 'not so remote from the realities of life', while striking idioms and expressions of English authors could be 'treasured up' for use in composition, after the method of learning classical languages. Robinson combined these rather old-fashioned utilitarian and rhetorical approaches with a belief in the moral and cultural importance of literature:

It is, however, in connection with what is called 'middle-class education' that the claims of English literature may be most effectively urged. In that literature, properly handled, we have a most valuable agency for the moral and intellectual culture of the professional classes. By means of that literature it seems to me that we might act very beneficially on the national mind, and do much to refine and invigorate the national character. ... The student will learn to appreciate the temper with which great minds approach the consideration of great questions; he will discover that truth is many-sided, that it is not identical or merely coextensive with individual opinion, and that the world is a good deal wider than his own set, party or class. And such a lesson the middle classes of this country greatly need. They are generally *honest* in their opinions, but in too many cases they are *narrow*.[11]

The great problem was how to convert the Philistines without making Barbarians of them: evidently the study of English literature had to be something more than merely a home-made version of the expensive classical education.

When three Royal Commissions within a decade showed a

[10] *Report of the Commission on the State of Popular Education*, 1861, Vol. I, p. 120.
[11] Rev. H. G. Robinson, 'On the Use of English Classical Literature', *Macmillan's Magazine*, Vol. II, pp. 425–33.

marked interest in the study of English, it was fast becoming an institution. And if Classics offered a ready model for organizing their poor relation, English studies were also being licked into shape by that invention of Victorian educators, the examination system. In 1855 a commission including Macaulay and Benjamin Jowett was set up to advise the Civil Service of the East India Company upon competitive entrance to the service; they recommended a written examination in a wide range of subjects, in which English was to be allotted the major proportion of possible marks:

Foremost among these subjects we place our own language and literature. One or more themes for English composition ought to be proposed. Two papers of questions ought to be set. One of these ought to be so framed as to enable the candidates to show their knowledge of the history and constitution of our country; the other ought to be so framed as to enable them to show the extent of their knowledge of our poets, wits, and philosophers.[12]

Those who were to take British rule overseas took with them also the British way of life, and their cultural heritage. This Civil Service examination had enormous influence on the schools, where candidates had to be prepared for the prescribed subjects. In 1867 the Taunton Commission heard G. W. Dasent explain how he examined such candidates in English literature:

I should take forty or fifty passages, selected from what I call fair authors—Shakespeare, Milton, Pope, and some of the later writers, Sir Walter Scott and Tennyson. I have set this question over and over again. 'Here is a passage. State where it comes from, explain any peculiarities of English in it, and state the context so far as you are able to do so.' If you set fifty passages, if the candidates are at all instructed, you will find that they answer it in various degrees. I remember an Irishman answering forty-five out of fifty right. I am sure I do not know how he did it. . . . If six or ten are answered it would be quite enough to show a considerable acquaintance with English literature.[13]

In its effects on teaching, nothing could have been more directly

---

[12] *Civil Service of the East India Company: Report to the Rt. Hon. Chas. Wood, M.P.*, 1855, p. 9.
[13] *Report of the Schools Enquiry Commission*, 1868, Vol. V, p. 521.

calculated to produce a mechanical grind of deadening fact and superficial understanding. Ironically, it was Dasent who had for a while succeeded F. D. Maurice as Professor of English Literature and History at King's College; from his evidence to the commission, he seems to have denied all that Maurice regarded as the sweetness and light of literature as a cultural education.

Matthew Arnold himself had been dismayed by the illiberal tendencies of the examination system, when in 1852, during his first year as a schools inspector, he reported on pupil-teachers:

I have been much struck in examining them towards the close of their apprenticeship, when they are generally at least eighteen years old, with the utter disproportion between the great amount of positive information and the low degree of mental culture and intelligence which they exhibit.

Queen's Scholarships for pupil-teachers were instituted in 1846, the Indian Civil Service examinations began in 1855, and the Oxford and Cambridge Local Examinations in 1858: English literature was an important subject in each of them. When the incorporeal University of London had been licensed in 1836, its general degree comprised four parts: Mathematics and Natural Philosophy; Chemistry, Animal Physiology, Vegetable Physiology, Structural Botany; Classics; and Logic and Moral Philosophy. The matriculation requirements included a qualification in English language, however, and in 1859 the first B.A. examination in English was held; we can see from the questions set in subsequent years that a memory for facts and the reiteration of the most elementary judgements were at a premium:

Describe briefly the plot of *Gorboduc*.

Who wrote *Gammer Gurton's Needle*, and when?
Trace briefly the plot.

Give the chief facts in the life of Shakespeare until 1603.

In 1871, shortly after Forster's Education Act had encouraged the expansion of elementary education, Matthew Arnold complained of the neglect of English in these schools:

What is comprised under the word literature is in itself the greatest

47

power available in education; of this power it is not too much to say that in our elementary schools at present no use is made at all.[14]

Perhaps as a result of this criticism, during the following year English literature was recognized as a class subject in the upper three grades of elementary schools. But the requirements were very mechanical; according to their age, pupils had to learn by heart 100, 200, or 300 lines of poetry, and to be able to explain the meaning and any allusions in the passage.

The proliferation in mid-century of examinations in English literature created a market for textbooks. Manuals and cyclopaedias of literary history were common, particularly of the crammer type, giving a chronological series of facts and dates, with potted biographies of the principal authors, and 'illustrations' in the form of selected passages from which the student could derive a hasty first-hand impression of the literature itself. When literary criticism was attempted, the compiler either was reduced to vague generalizations that could be vaguely imitated, or resorted to quotation from a recognized authority, usually Hallam or Lord Macaulay. Two of the earliest of these outlines were, however, better than many successors: in 1844 there first appeared Robert Chambers's *Cyclopaedia of English Literature*, which in later editions has drawn upon the contributions of distinguished scholars, and in the same year Charles Knight published G. C. Craik's *Sketches of Literature and Learning in England*. But the misplaced pedantry and unimaginative approach which too often characterized these manuals can be sampled in a passage from Joseph Payne's *Studies in English Poetry*, an anthology for schools published in 1845; Payne is here elucidating Hamlet's famous soliloquy:

'Sea of troubles'—Pope proposed to alter this into 'a siege of troubles', upon which Mr. Knight, in his pictorial edition, remarks, 'surely the metaphor of *sea* to denote an overwhelming flood of troubles, is highly beautiful'. This is unquestionable. The difficulty however lies in the expression '*to take arms* against a sea', which, strictly speaking, presents an incongruous image. If we consider the words 'a sea' as unemphatic,

14 See W. F. Connell, *The Educational Thought and Influence of Matthew Arnold*, 1950, pp. 180–2.

48

and merely used for 'a host' or great number, the whole will be harmonised.[15]

Often alongside the desiccated literary history were purple-passages in the Romantic manner, like this paragraph from a Scottish textbook of 1853, William Spalding's *History of English Literature*:

Spenser's eye dwelt, with fond and untiring admiration, on the gorgeous scenery which covered the elfin-land of knighthood and romance: present realities passed before him unseen, or were remembered only to be woven insensibly into the gossamer-tissue of fantasy; and, lost in his life-long dream of antique grandeur and ideal loveliness, he was blind to all the phenomena of that renovated world, which was rising around him out of the ancient chaos.[16]

These excerpts suggest that the ability to blend scholarship and literary judgement, as in the best kind of modern academic writing, took some time to evolve; the authors of these early textbooks went back to the available modes of literary discussion, and either adopted the tone of a Hazlitt or lapsed into the heavy editorial manner of a textual commentary. Austin Dobson's *Civil Service Handbook of English Literature*, which appeared in 1874, did not differ appreciably in conception or quality from its predecessors. But in view of the kind of examinations for which these books were designed, they probably served their purpose well enough.

More successful and important, on the whole, were the texts edited and annotated for students by specially-commissioned scholars. The Macmillan brothers were amongst the first in this field, with their 'Golden Treasury' series and 'Globe' editions. For this firm W. G. Clark and W. Aldis Wright commemorated the tercentenary of Shakespeare's birth by producing the 'Globe' Shakespeare in 1864, a text of the canon which is still in general usage for most purposes of convenient reference. Aldis Wright, who succeeded Clark as Librarian of Trinity College, Cambridge, in particular established new standards of accurate scholarship: in his own authoritative words, 'Ignorance and conceit are the fruitful parents of conjectural emendation'. His edition of Bacon's

---

[15] J. Payne, *Studies in English Poetry* (3rd edn. 1856), p. 276.
[16] W. Spalding, *History of English Literature*, 1853, p. 203.

Essays for the 'Golden Treasury' series in 1862 anticipated the 'new bibliography' of the twentieth century by indicating the possible existence of variations between different copies of the same edition of an Elizabethan text. The presses of the ancient universities, too, helped to supply the increasing demand for students' editions: the Clarendon Press series began in 1866, and the Pitt Press series in 1875. By 1887, *Low's Educational Catalogue* listed some 280 school editions of English literature, exclusive of Shakespeare.

No one was more industrious in this field than Henry Morley, whose *First Sketch of English Literature* sold over 30,000 copies between 1873 and 1898. In 1883 he was invited by Routledge & Son to edit a new series of shilling volumes, to be known as *Morley's Universal Library*, and sixty-three monthly volumes were produced during the next five years. Meanwhile Cassells secured his services in 1885 to re-edit their *National Library*, a cheap weekly series.

To Henry Morley belongs the distinction of being the first to devote an academic career in England solely to English studies, if we except Masson, whose last thirty years were spent in Scotland. For nearly forty years Morley held university posts connected with the teaching of English literature: with him English studies became fully professional, and by the end of his career we are almost in the modern period. His successor at University College in 1889 was W. P. Ker, and in the year of his death, 1894, the Oxford English School was established. Morley's career is worth recounting, not only because it spans the last half of the century, but also because in his prodigious and varied activity he crossed most of the paths we have been following through the period.

After training as a medical student at King's College, London, between 1838 and 1843, school-teaching in Manchester and Liverpool, and entering journalism for a short time (during which he impressed Dickens with his work for *Household Words*), Morley began his major career in 1857 when he was appointed to teach English in the new evening classes at King's College. He had previously, in 1852, considered offering himself as a candidate for the English Chair at University College, when it was vacated by

Clough, but had decided to wait until he was more certain of success. This was to come when David Masson, who had been appointed there in 1852, left in 1865 to become Professor of Rhetoric and Belles Lettres in Edinburgh.

Morley's experience in the evening classes assured him of his ability as a lecturer at the same time as it determined his bent as a literary historian. During his first year at King's College, he recorded his early triumph enthusiastically in his diary:

On Tuesday, March 16, my winter course of lectures ended at King's College, and I received twenty-one guineas and some odd shillings as my share of the fees. The lectures, which began in October, have been so planned as to embrace, with a more particular study of Spenser and Dryden, a general view of the development of our language and literature from the earliest of its days to the year 1700. They have so far succeeded with the students that I am asked to form a summer class. . . . I have enjoyed very much the delivery of the literature lectures, and the class has stuck by me so steadily that I expect next winter to find its borders enlarged, because I hope instead of three to have a dozen men who follow up the subject through a second course. Furnivall, who lectures upon English at the Working Men's College, dropped in upon my last lecture but one, which happened to be a mere clearance of scraps, etc.,—no lecture at all. He admired the earnest working manner of the men, but said, 'my pace was killing'. I know, however, of old, by my own experience as a student, that quick lectures are followed much more easily than slow ones. We have felt our way along, and I have known that the class followed me, while it is very certain that I have been able to include in the course at least one third more information than there would have been room to get into it had I preferred a dignified walk to a sharp trot over the ground.[17]

Morley continued to prefer the sharp trot, and covered extensive tracts of English literature with those classes in the course of the next eight years. He was soon writing a comprehensive history of English literature, the first part of which appeared in 1864. *The History of English Writers* grew out of his work for the evening classes, and carried the story from the 'origins' as far as Chaucer. The opening chapters of a second volume, continuing to Dunbar, were published in 1867, but by this time he had left King's

[17] H. S. Solly, *The Life of Henry Morley, LL.D.*, 1898, p. 231.

College to become Professor of English Language and Literature at University College.

The appointment was made in 1865, and when he assumed his duties there were over 300 students in the Faculty of Arts and Law, of whom fifty-two were studying English. These figures rose throughout the succeeding years, reaching over 100 in 1872, after which a slight decline was offset in 1878 by the admission of women: the university having received a supplementary charter allowing it to confer degrees on women. With 191 students in the English course that year, the numbers rose above 200 during 1879 and 1880, but thereafter they began to decrease, until in 1888, Morley's final year at the college, there were only 109.

A former pupil of his at University College between 1869 and 1874, describing Morley's approach to his subject, referred to his 'essentially Teutonic quality of massive earnestness'. He wrote in 1881 of his belief in the value of his subject, in terms similar to those of Thomas Dale and F. D. Maurice:

> . . . the chief use to my mind of a study of English literature is to sustain the spiritual side of life, and it has been, at any rate, my chief aim so to teach it as to bring it into use as a natural corrective to the materialist tendencies of the age.[18]

However, Morley's scholarship was more formidable than that of his predecessors, and like A. J. Scott, he perceived the value of literature as a record of civilization. When he became an examiner for the University of London in 1878, it was his policy to make the prescribed period of English literature coincident with the historical period to be studied. This policy reflected his conviction, expressed in the preface to his *First Sketch of English Literature* (1873), that 'the political and social history of England should be studied along with any chosen period of its literature, while direct acquaintance should be made with one or two of the best books of that period'.

In the light of this thorough-going historical bias, which threatens to subordinate literature to other interests, it is rather surprising that Morley also held by the moral agency of literature.

[18] H. S. Solly, op. cit., p. 330.

There is indeed something of a missionary fervour about his career, for apart from his duties at University College, he gave many courses of popular lectures in London and the provinces between 1869 and 1878. In the days before such ventures were subsidized, Morley's success showed that they could be made to pay. Perhaps the most striking example of his unflagging industry is an entry in his diary from this period: the bizarre mixture of literary giants and railway timetables catches something of the atmosphere of his professional mission:

Wednesday: To Hitchin 1.10: On with Wordsworth, Byron, Montgomery, and Campbell. Leave 5.16; leave Peterborough 7.12, Darlington 11.33.

Thursday: Darlington 12: John Locke's Philosophy. Leave 1.40, Redcar 2.40; or leave 2.40, Redcar 4.40, Redcar 6.30: Later Elizabethan Dramatists—Dekker, Chapman, Marston, etc. Leave Redcar 8, Stockton 8.45: Shakespeare's Comedies, Merchant of Venice.

Friday: Leave Stockton 6.30. York: Dryden; Defoe's Early Writings. Leave York, London and N.W., 12.40, via Leeds; Liverpool 4.15. Lecture New Brighton 8: Ideal Commonwealths. Leave Lime Street 11 p.m.; Birmingham 2.30.

Saturday: Leave Birmingham 7.30. Reading carriage slipped 9.30, Lecture 11: Jeremy Taylor. Leave Reading 12.45, Moorgate Street 2.20, Fenchurch Street 3.10, Leytonstone 3.45: Richardson, Fielding. and Smollett.[19]

The imagination boggles at all this: how much, for example, could be said about Richardson, Fielding, and Smollett in an hour's lecture? A sharp trot over the ground indeed. Such was his incredible energy, that when Morley finally gave up his strenuous commitments as lecturer and examiner in 1888, it was only to immerse himself more fully in the business of editing and annotating scores of literary texts.

Until 1880 Morley's English classes at University College grew steadily larger, while in King's College the Department of General Literature and Science had gradually fallen into decline. The rot began to set in at mid-century, when the college could

19 Ibid., p. 297.

no longer maintain its position as a half-way house between the public schools and Oxford, Cambridge, or the professions. Classics were losing their appeal, and the schools themselves were improving and preparing their own candidates for the universities and the Civil Service.

In 1852 certain reforms were therefore made in the curriculum of the department: the proportion of Classics and mathematics was reduced, and lectures on history and literature were increased from two to four hours a week. Moreover, classes on English composition, never before taught in the college, were now introduced to give the course a more practical bias. But the number of day-students in the department continued to go down: from 106 in 1853, there were only fifty-eight in 1866. The evening classes, which started in 1855, at first proved more successful; when Morley came to teach the English class in 1857, there were altogether 378 evening students, and when he left in 1865 the total in these classes had risen to 654. But by 1883 the numbers had fallen to 384, while in the next year there were a mere thirty-nine day-students in the General Department.[20] During these years the Chair of English Literature and History had two occupants. J. S. Brewer, who came to King's College in 1839 as a lecturer in Classics, was made assistant to F. D. Maurice in 1851, and, after the brief tenure of G. W. Dasent, succeeded to the Chair in 1855. Brewer was a friend and admirer of Maurice, and later himself became Principal of the Working Men's College. His main contribution to learning was made as a historian of early sixteenth-century England, though he was consulted by the Clarendon Press in drawing up their plans for publishing a series of English classics: he died before this project was completed. When he resigned from the Chair in 1877, his place was taken by J. W. Hales, whose interests lay more in language than in literature, as we might infer from his essay on 'The Teaching of English'. For some years Hales was Professor of English in two colleges, for he did not give up his duties in Bedford College until 1890; he remained at King's College until 1903.

The diminution which both the original London colleges began

---

[20] F. J. C. Hearnshaw, *A Centenary History of King's College, London*, 1929, pp. 301–10.

to suffer in the 1880's had two principal causes, both of them external: the creation in 1876 of the London Society for the Extension of University Teaching, and the opening of new 'civic' colleges. While in London the extra-mural activities of F. D. Maurice and a few of his colleagues from King's College anticipated the coming of University Extension proper, the movement was given fresh impetus in the provinces during the late 1860's. The name of James Stuart, the Cambridge don who gave a series of scientific lectures in midland and northern towns in 1867, will always be closely associated with the origins of University Extension, since the success of his experiment encouraged the organization of a regular Extension system by the University of Cambridge in 1873. In the meantime, however, extra-mural courses of an informal kind were being given simultaneously from other centres; according to Henry Morley,

In 1868 Ladies' Educational Associations were formed in several towns of Lancashire and Yorkshire for bringing teachers from the Scottish or English Universities to give courses of about ten lectures to women only. In the same year, but, I think, a few months later, such a Ladies' Educational Association was established in Edinburgh. Professor Masson gave a course upon some subject in English Literature, and another of the Edinburgh University professors gave a science course. The lectures were to ladies' classes, which were formed and controlled by this association as an independent agency outside the University. The example of Edinburgh was, in another month or two, followed in London, where there was formed a Ladies' Educational Association that also began with two courses—one in science, one in literature—which were given by Professor Carey Foster and by me at the Beethoven Rooms in Harley Street. These courses opened in March 1869.[21]

The demand for Extension courses also came from Mechanics' Institutes, and when the Nottingham Mechanics' Institution held 'a large meeting of Representative Working Men' in 1871 to assess the demand for regular instruction, there were four subjects 'which they considered of the greatest importance and interest to them, namely—Political Economy, The Science of Health, The Constitutional History of England, and English Literature'. This

21 H. S. Solly, op. cit., p. 263.

was reported in their petition to Cambridge University in 1873:

that, as the great bulk of the youth of the nation cannot go to them, the Universities should send out teachers whom they had trained and equipped for the service of the nation. It was felt that in this way the Universities would then hold a position and have an immediate influence in every part of the country, and the great mass of the people would be led to value them as national institutions, directly benefitting them with the high advantage of knowledge and culture.[22]

Similar appeals came from other mechanics' institutes and local associations for the education of women, and Cambridge acceded to the request. Five years later, and two years after the London Extension Society was formed, the Oxford Extension Scheme began in 1878, when the Oxford Association for the Higher Education of Women was also founded. The two ancient universities were beginning to assume some responsibility for the teaching of English literature.

The success of these Extension schemes soon led to the foundation of university colleges in several large industrial towns of the north and midlands, namely at Leeds (1874), Sheffield (1879), Birmingham (1880), Liverpool (1881), and Nottingham (1881). But first of these provincial colleges was Owens College, founded in Manchester in 1850.

Like later institutions in the north of England, Owens College was the result of a combination of civic pride and the private endowments of local industrial wealth. Though the idea of a university college had been mooted much earlier, it was the benefaction of John Owens that first enabled a college to be established and in 1851 the Queen's Warrant was obtained permitting certificates to be granted which qualified students for the degree examination of London University. When A. J. Scott came from University College he was not only the first Principal of the new college: he was also Professor of Comparative Grammar, of English Language and Literature, of Logic, and of Mental and Moral Philosophy. Not surprisingly, he found these multiple duties too heavy before long, and in 1857 he resigned his office as Principal,

22 J. A. H. Green, *History of the Nottingham Mechanics' Institution, 1837–1887*, 1887, pp. 33–34.

though he did not retire from teaching until 1866. The plurality of Scott's professorships is an indication of the elementary level of instruction which was the reality behind their rather grandiose titles. In English, for example, a committee appointed by Owens's trustees to define the studies laid stress entirely on the grammatical discipline, 'the accuracy of language which is essential to the accuracy of reasoning'. So thought those hard-headed Manchester men, but after the first full session, their professors reported that the city's secondary education was so poor that the students were unable to benefit from a university training. A. J. Scott told the first annual assembly of parents and teachers:

It is evident that you can have no college, unless you have schools which actually do prepare for college. Should we fix a standard which the schools afforded no means of attaining, we might close our doors. Should we directly undertake the higher school education, we should rather compete with the schools than fulfil the proper destination of a college.[23]

Consequently in the following year special classes were started in Classics and mathematics for schoolmasters. Evening classes were also opened, and figures for the year 1856-7 showed that English Literature was by far the most popular subject.

But when Greenwood took over the office of Principal from Scott in 1857, public reaction in the city towards the college was concerned and critical. It was felt that classical and humane studies occupied too much of the curriculum, which should have been made more representative of the trades and sciences characteristic of the locality. The *Manchester Guardian* described the college as 'a mortifying failure' in June 1858. Principal Greenwood's reply to utilitarian criticism was contained in his annual report, presented in July 1858. He produced statistics to show that Manchester allotted a much shorter period for the education of its youth than other comparable cities. In this same year, the college rejected a proposal that it should be converted into a teachers' training college, and it received the permission of London University to hold the B.A. examination on its own premises. During the next session, a

[23] J. Thompson, *The Owens College: its Foundation and Growth*, 1886, pp. 141-3. See also H. B. Charlton, *Portrait of a University 1851-1951*, 1951, p. 29.

higher number of students enrolled and 'the average number of classes attended by each day student was four against two and a half last session, and by each evening student two as against one and a quarter last session.'

It seemed as though the early critical period was over. Three years later, in 1861, Greenwood was instrumental in amalgamating the Manchester Working Men's College with Owens College for systematized evening classes on the model of King's College in London. The total number of evening students consequently rose to 235, from 102 in the previous session. English language and literature was taught in these classes by the Rev. W. Gaskell, husband of the novelist, who had been associated with the Manchester Working Men's College since its foundation in 1858.

In keeping with the expansion of the college, and following the reform in the old London general degree, the courses were divided into Arts and Sciences in 1863. Relations with the city seemed to have improved as the college became more successful, for in the same year the municipal authorities resolved that the tercentenary of the birth of Shakespeare 'would be most fitly commemorated in Manchester by the foundation of two scholarships, to be called "Shakespere Scholarships", for the promotion of the study of English language and literature, in connection with Owens College and the Free Grammar School'. Overcrowding now compelled the college to find an extension, and two Acts of Parliament in 1870 and 1871 respectively provided the new Owens Extension College with a public constitution of senate and council to replace the government by trustees, and amalgamated it with the old Owens College. The new constitution admitted women to the courses, but it was not until 1877 that a women's college was opened, to be finally incorporated as a department of Owens College in 1883.

There was a growing antipathy among the professors to the constraint imposed upon them by the examination requirements dictated from London. Consequently, in 1876 a committee was appointed by council to examine the possibility of seeking a University Charter. A press campaign, the lobbying of influential people, and a deputation to the Government in 1877 provoked the

jealousies of other northern colleges, which would have preferred a university incorporating several colleges, not the monopoly of one. In 1880, therefore, the federated Victoria University
was granted a charter, its seat being in Manchester. Owens College
was admitted immediately, Liverpool in 1884, and the Yorkshire
College, Leeds, in 1887.

Adolphus William Ward had succeeded A. J. Scott as Professor of English Language and Literature in 1866. In 1875 he
persuaded the senate to combine the Chair of English Literature
with that of History, and to create a separate Lectureship in English Language. T. N. Toller was appointed to this Lectureship, and
in 1880 he became the first Smith Professor of English Language.
Ward's administrative skill was invaluable to Owens College as
it was preparing for university status, and his colleague T. F. Tout,
the historian, later wrote of him that 'he was never more happy
than when discharging the duties of the president of a learned
body'. A contemporary of Masson and Morley, he was like them
a literary historian, charting the vast seas of English literature.
In 1875 he published a *History of English Dramatic Literature to the
Death of Queen Anne*, a two-volume work which he enlarged and
reissued in 1899. He had retired from Owens College and returned
to Cambridge in 1896, and, encouraged by the success of the
Cambridge Modern History of which he was joint editor, he undertook the editorship of the *Cambridge History of English Literature* in
1907. Undiluted literary history, however, is not very lively
material for lectures to students, and when the young Walter
Raleigh deputized for Ward at Owens College in 1889, he
formed a gloomy impression of the state of English studies there.
Raleigh found that all that was required of him was the imparting
of facts, in great quantities, to students whose unimaginative and
mechanical expectations were unable to digest anything else:

They do not understand it all. They blink at it. I made some remarks
on Poetry in general which cost me more than fifteen matter of fact
lectures, and they laid down their pens and smiled from an infinite
height.

So I must just boil down text books in the recognized fashion. It is
very good of Professor Ward to lend me all his MS. lectures, for

from a study of them, I have been compelled to think but poorly of them.[24]

Raleigh of course allowed himself a liberty of comment in his private letters that would have been out of place in another context, but his observations not only reveal the familiar arrogance of a young lecturer towards the old-fashioned methods of his professor: they contain a radical indictment of the cramping examination system:

I am sorry to say I have very strong opinions about the futility of the method of education in vogue at all these places. They are all governed by men of business whose idea is that *business* should go on there all day. They turn out no *men* here on the Arts side. I grind along and do my work, but the system is a wicked one—or would be if stupidity permitted.

George Gissing had been a student at Owens College, and he later recreated the spirit of the place under the pseudonym of 'Whitelaw College' in the first chapter of his novel *Born in Exile*. The immaturity of the students, the blind desire for education and self-improvement as a road to opportunity in a materialist world, and the consequent shibboleths of examinations and diplomas, all described in Gissing's best drab manner, corroborate Raleigh's impressions. It was this state of affairs which afforded some grounds for the fears of those academic conservatives in Oxford, who withstood the demands for the recognition of English literature as an object of serious study with the argument that it too easily deteriorated into 'a cram-school'. No less did it convince others, however, of the necessity of making Oxford and Cambridge 'national' universities, and of establishing English studies there in order to promote and preserve better standards of teaching and scholarship.

Meanwhile, much that has been said of Owens College was true of the other civic colleges. The Yorkshire College of Science was opened in Leeds in 1874; as the name implies, the studies were at first wholly technical and scientific, particularly as they related to local industries. In 1877, however, when Owens College showed

[24] *Letters of Sir Walter Raleigh, 1876–1922*, ed. Lady Raleigh, 2 vols., 1926, i. 122 *et seq.*

signs of moving towards university status, the Yorkshire College of Science made a politic concession to the pressure from Extension schemes in the city, and Professors of Classics and of Modern Literature and History were appointed, Cyril Ransome being the latter. Consequently, in the following year the college was renamed simply as the Yorkshire College. But the new professors in the Arts department remained in an inferior position: their salaries were smaller, and their function was merely to prepare science students for general or subsidiary courses, since no part of the syllabus led to an Arts degree. The preponderance of technical subjects, in fact, handicapped the Yorkshire College's move to enter Victoria University; but when the college was finally affiliated in 1887, the position of the Arts faculty gradually improved. A. J. Grant, a popular Extension lecturer, succeeded to the Chair of Modern Literature and History in 1896, and in the same year the minimum age of entry was raised from fifteen to sixteen. Evidently the academic standard was not very high, for although the college doubled its numbers from about 400 in 1887 to over 800 in 1903, most of the students took pass degrees: a mere half-dozen honours degrees was the total in Arts by 1904.[25]

In Sheffield, Firth College grew directly from the Cambridge Extension courses. The founder, Mark Firth, had been responsible for bringing Extension lecturers to the city, during his term as Mayor in 1875. 'Being convinced of the benefits resulting from the lectures and classes', in the words of his deed of settlement, Firth conferred his college upon the city in 1879. One of the original lecturers was his nephew, Charles Harding Firth, who later became the Regius Professor of Modern History in Oxford, and a champion of English studies there. The first course in English literature at Firth College was an evening class of the Extension type, started in 1881 by P. A. Barnett, Professor of Literature and History. The college was too small to gain admittance to Victoria University, and when it received a government grant of the princely sum of £1,200 in 1889, it was decided to use the money to appoint a Professor of English Literature, whose duties were to include supervising the expansion of the college's Extension

[25] A. N. Shimmin, *The University of Leeds: The First Half Century*, 1954, pp. 1–23.

schemes. H. W. Appleton, who had been Lecturer in Classics, was made the first Professor of English Language, Literature, and History; in 1896 the duties were divided so that Appleton taught history, while English studies were taken over by a former Extension lecturer, G. C. Moore Smith.[26]

University College, Liverpool, was another inspiration of civic pride. A town meeting held there in 1878 declared that 'Liverpool ought not to be behind Manchester, Sheffield, Leeds, Nottingham, and Bristol in a movement of such importance as that of providing for the higher education of youths after leaving school'. The college opened in January 1882, when the minimum age for entry was fifteen, with an entrance examination for those under sixteen. The first Professor of Modern Literature and History was A. C. Bradley.[27]

The two colleges at Birmingham, Queen's and Mason, were at first predominantly scientific. Queen's College had a religious qualification in its entrance requirements, while Mason, which opened in 1880, was defiantly utilitarian in spirit, 'to the exclusion of mere literary education or theology'. The medical department of Queen's was transferred to Mason in 1892, and later Queen's became wholly a theological college. When Mason College was extended in 1881, however, a Faculty of Arts was created, with Professors of English and Classics, and lecturers in French and German. Anglo-Saxon studies came under the auspices of the German department. The first Professor of English was Edward Arber, who had been one of Morley's students in the King's College evening classes, and later in 1879 left the Civil Service to become his assistant at University College. Arber was a specialist: his interests were primarily in the sixteenth and seventeenth centuries, and he did much valuable, if not altogether meticulous, work in editing texts useful to scholars as well as undergraduates. Apart from preparing the thirty volumes of *Arber's English Reprints* and the sixteen volumes of the *English Scholar's Library*, he transcribed the *Registers of the Company of Stationers* (*1554-1640*) in five volumes between 1875 and 1894, edited the *Term Cata-*

[26] A. W. Chapman, *The Story of a Modern University*, 1955, pp. 13–81.
[27] *University College, Liverpool. Calendar for Session 1882–83*, Preface.

logues (1668-1709) in three volumes between 1903 and 1906, and compiled *An English Garner* of broadsheet ballads, pamphlets, and other more ephemeral literature of the Elizabethan and Stuart periods. His rabid Protestantism, however, gave a rather eccentric twist to his literary judgements.[28]

The first Professor of Language and Literature at University College, Nottingham, in 1881, was the Rev. J. E. Symes, who had instructed Nottingham Extension classes in literature and history since 1875. He appears to have been an old-fashioned follower of the Christian Socialists, and later his political views were to cause friction with the municipal committee which governed the college, particularly after he had taken the chair at a public meeting addressed by William Morris. His duties in the college embraced responsibility for the whole of the Arts department, including the teaching of political economy and history, as well as English. As this implies, the academic standard was very elementary, and the college functioned more as a school than as a university, by preparing students for the London Matriculation and the Cambridge Locals.[29]

Although the University of Durham was founded in 1832, and was thus the first university outside Oxford and Cambridge to confer its own degrees, I have left it out of account so far because its ecclesiastical bias made it a special case. Classics and theology were the principal studies, and no systematic course in English was provided until the end of the century. A proposal was made in 1846 to create a Readership of Anglo-Saxon and Old English Literature, but nothing came of it. In 1882 the Rev. H. J. R. Marston was made a Reader in English Literature; his duties were to give two public lectures in each of the two winter terms, but interest flagged and the Readership was discontinued in 1889. In that year, Henry Ellershaw became a Lecturer in Classics; he eventually taught some English and in 1910 was made the first Professor of English Language and Literature. Attached to the University of Durham, however, was Armstrong (later King's) College in Newcastle, founded in 1871 to house the department of

---

[28] E. W. Vincent and P. Hinton, *The University of Birmingham*, 1947, p. 65.
[29] A. C. Wood, *A History of University College, Nottingham, 1881–1948*, 1953, pp. 25–40.

science, and much more akin to the civic universities in spirit. There in 1886 Alfred Paton was made Professor of Classics and English, to supervise the preliminary requirements for the science degree. In 1895 Armstrong College won the first round of a battle with the Arts Faculty in Durham over the question of compulsory Greek, and created a new tripos degree of B.Litt., which included more advanced studies in English literature and modern languages. The college continued to confer degrees in letters but not in arts until 1909.[30]

By the 1880's, then, English studies were in a curious state. They were expanding rapidly, but the expansion was only lateral, within the lower levels of the academic hierarchy. And, as is often the case with hasty developments, the foundations were ramshackle and lacked proper co-ordination. The study of English literature was attached on the one hand to history, which gave it a framework of scholarship and knowledge about literature; on the other hand, it took its informing spirit from Classics, as an instrument of cultural education on a parallel but much broader social plane. Moreover the old ties between 'literature' and 'language' survived the waning of rhetorical studies by including within their scope Old English, as a study both historical and, like Classics, philological. English studies were in a state of flux, not that there was anything disastrous in these multiple and sometimes conflicting influences. On the contrary, they greatly enriched and stimulated the subject, and have continued to do so. But the principal danger was a lack of balance, a flux in which the real controlling agency was the examination system, which, as Matthew Arnold and after him Walter Raleigh complained, too often stifled the real interest and value of the subject. The function of English studies as part of a general humane education had now to be reconciled with the need for properly-trained teachers: very few of the first professors were themselves trained in English; they were either ministers of religion or recruited from journalism. Later, many of them came into English Studies from Oxford 'Greats', among them A. C. Bradley, Oliver Elton, Ernest de Selincourt, John Nichol at Glasgow, and Churton Collins. The

[30] C. E. Whiting, *The University of Durham 1832–1932*, 1932, p. 143.

early progress of English studies is reflected in the origins of its teachers. But, if academic standards were to be raised, and they stood in sore need of some improvement, then facilities for further study and research-training were called for. In short, somewhere a School of English had to be created with the necessary authority to realize the true potentialities of the subject and to give a lead to the rest of the country. An academic subject is never at a stand-still, it is always moving in one or more directions; to one observer at least it seemed clear that English studies were moving in the wrong direction by the 1880's:

To all appearances, indeed, there is no branch of education in a more flourishing condition or more full of promise for the future. But, un-happily, this is very far from being the case. In spite of its great vogue, and in spite of the time and energy lavished in teaching it, no fact is more certain than that from an educational point of view it is, and from the very first has been, an utter failure. Teachers perceive with per-plexity that it attains none of the ends which a subject in itself so full of attraction and interest might be expected to attain. It fails, they com-plain, to fertilize; it fails to inform; it fails even to awake curiosity. For a dozen youths who derive real benefit from the instruction they get in preparing for an examination in History there are not two who derive the smallest benefit from the instruction they get in preparing for an examination in Literature.[31]

A crisis was surely imminent; and John Churton Collins, if any-one, was the man to precipitate it.

[31] J. C. Collins, *The Study of English Literature*, 1891, p. 17.

V

THE REFORM MOVEMENT IN OXFORD

WHEN the Nottingham Mechanics' Institution petitioned the University of Cambridge in 1873 for a regular Extension Scheme, they spoke of the two ancient universities thus becoming 'national institutions', where teachers could be 'trained and equipped for the service of the nation'. This plain and perhaps not wholly ingenuous suggestion touched upon the most delicate issue in the politics of nineteenth-century Oxford and Cambridge. To whom did the universities belong: to the colleges or to the nation? In the movement for reform, they were not only subject to pressure from outside, and public exposure of their inadequacies, but also divided within their own walls by sharp differences of opinion on their true traditions and future policies. Even those who agreed that Oxford and Cambridge should be made 'national institutions', differed in their interpretations of what that implied: the extent to which the universities should retain responsibility for their own affairs, and the nature of reforms in teaching methods, curricula, and university government, were issues liable to inflame the academic passions and provoke in men of learning the ugly spirit of faction and prejudice. There were also, of course, those obscurantists who maintained that the unreformed universities as they stood, with their religious tests and the privilege of antiquated statutes, were already meeting whatever claim the nation had in justice upon them. Nevertheless, the reforms came in a gradual sequence throughout the century, and the movement of the 1880's to establish a School of English Studies in Oxford was only one aspect of a more extensive, protracted, and hard-fought revolution.

The picture of late eighteenth-century Oxford, in its intellectual torpor and academic stagnation, is familiar enough, and whatever minor qualifications may be made, the main features are those of an inefficient and outworn system of education. One cause of this state of affairs was the lack of co-ordination between the studies at school and those in the university: to many able pupils, like Gibbon, Bentham, and Southey, the college teaching offered little that was new or beyond what they had already mastered. As late as 1855, according to Mark Pattison, an undergraduate from a good school 'finds that in exchanging lesson for lecture he has gone back a couple of years in the standard of requirement'. Even so, matters had begun to improve as a result of the new Examination Statutes introduced during the first half of the century. The formal requirements for taking the first degree had dwindled into little more than a pantomime during the eighteenth century, but in 1800 the Public Examination Statute introduced a new oral examination in grammar, rhetoric, logic, moral philosophy, and the elements of mathematics and physics. The candidate was to be allowed a choice in the number of books on which he elected to be examined, 'but always and for every degree, an examination in Humane Literature is to be set on foot, and especially one in the Greek and Roman writers, three of whom at the fewest, of the best age and stamp, are to be used'. A statute of 1807 modified these arrangements by introducing a written examination for the Honours School, and separating mathematics and physics from the requirements *in Literis Humanioribus*. A further reform was made in 1830, when ancient history was included with rhetoric, poetry, and moral and political science. Oxford was following that general movement in classical studies away from the purely linguistic study of ancient texts and literary facility in verse composition, towards a study of the substance of texts, and of the subjects themselves. In 1850, the classical examination was divided into two parts, Moderations and *Literae Humaniores*, so that after studying the literature and language, the student could devote himself to philosophy and ancient history. Each of these statutes grew out of its predecessor: by introducing subjects of examination as well as texts, they facilitated an extension by which in the future more subjects could be included, independent of the classical authorities.[1]

[1] M. L. Clarke, *Classical Education in Great Britain, 1500–1900*, 1959, pp. 98–113.

Meanwhile Oxford had to contend with severe and radical criticism from outside. In 1809, the *Edinburgh Review* launched an attack on the exclusively classical curriculum, and upon the provincial obscurity of Oxford scholarship. In July, an edition of Strabo published by the University Press was castigated as a 'ponderous monument of operose ignorance and vain expense', and the onslaught was sustained in the next issue, when a review of R. L. Edgeworth's *Essays on Professional Education* was made the occasion for a general diatribe on Oxford education:

The English Clergy, in whose hands education entirely rests, bring up the first young men of the country, as if they were all to keep grammar schools in little country towns; and a nobleman, upon whose knowledge and liberality the honour and welfare of his country may depend, is diligently worried, for half his life, with the small pedantry of longs and shorts.[2]

Oxford found its champion in Edward Copleston, Fellow of Oriel College and himself one of the new reformers. Copleston, who published his *Reply to the Calumnies of the Edinburgh Review* in 1810, rested his defence upon the value of Classics as a general humane education, and upon the duty of the university

to send out into the world an annual supply of men, whose minds are imbued with literature according to their several measures of capacity, impressed with what we hold to be the soundest principles of policy and religion, grounded in the elements of science, and taught how they may best direct their efforts to further attainments in that line.[3]

That Oxford had few scholars of European reputation, or that the university contributed little to the furthering of knowledge, was to Copleston and his party of little concern, since in their view the process of educating undergraduates was the university's prime function. As Thomas Gaisford, the Regius Professor of Greek, asserted with sublime arrogance, the study of Greek literature 'not only elevates above the vulgar herd, but leads not infrequently to positions of considerable emolument'.[4]

This preliminary skirmishing was followed in 1831 by Sir

[2] *Edinburgh Review*, No. XXVIII, Art. X, pp. 429–41; No. XXIX, Art. III, pp. 40–53.
[3] C. E. Mallet, *A History of the University of Oxford*, 3 vols., 1927, iii. 184.
[4] See G. Faber, *Jowett, A Portrait with a Background*, 1957, p. 222.

William Hamilton's full-scale assault, once again through the columns of the *Edinburgh Review*, in which he accused the colleges of having usurped the power and prerogatives of the university. The public teaching of faculty professors, he alleged, had in the course of time given way to the private monopolies of college interests, so that only elementary tuition was available and the tutors were not always appointed for their abilities in special fields of study. 'The present capacity of the University to effect the purposes of its establishment', he wrote, 'must, consequently, be determined by the capacity of each fellow tutor to compass the encyclopaedia of academical instruction.'[5] Hamilton cast the colleges in a villainous rôle, and made into a dramatic conspiracy what had been in fact more of an accidental process in the evolution of college teaching to supplement the inadequacies of the old Regents system. Nevertheless his criticism of the weakness in the college system must be admitted as valid. No doubt it was partly as a result of this development that few professors during the eighteenth century had shown much zeal in claiming lost privileges, or indeed in exercising any of their duties at all.

The reformers therefore wanted to see an adjustment of college interests to permit an expansion of professorial responsibility and to give a stronger hand to the faculties. The colleges were naturally alarmed, not only because their self-interest was involved, but because they were threatened with interference from outside; and in fact the Laudian statutes had undergone considerable revision by 1850, when Lord John Russell announced the appointment of a Royal Commission to inquire into the systems of education in both the ancient universities. Many who were not unsympathetic to proposals which came from reformers inside the university, deeply resented the prospect of changes imposed by Act of Parliament, and the Hebdomadal Board issued a haughty defence of the antiquated Laudian statutes, that really belied their own previous piecemeal reforms. 'In 1636', said the Board,

the University revised the whole body of its statutes, and the academic system of study was admirably arranged at a time when not only the nature and faculties of the human mind were exactly what they are

[5] *Edinburgh Review*, No. CVI, Art. VI, pp. 384–427.

still, and must of course remain, but the principles also of sound and enlarged intellectual culture were far from being imperfectly understood.[6]

It was an attitude of supercilious defiance which Oxford often adopted in the face of any suggestion that she could not properly manage her own affairs. In the view of her critics, however, Oxford's affairs were too closely bound up with those of the nation to permit the university to go her own sweet way, and no doubt the idea of a 'national university' was largely inspired by the new spirit of German education, in which specialized professorial teaching and schools of research figured so prominently. As a result of the Royal Commissions of 1850 and 1872, and the consequent parliamentary legislation, far-reaching changes were effected in the ancient universities. In Oxford, the professoriate was strengthened by finances converted from college fellowships, and its position reinforced by representation in the reconstituted Hebdomadal Council. The clerical monopoly of university affairs was further reduced by the institution of the House of Congregation for resident M.A.'s, and by the admission of nonconformists to matriculation and the first degree. New faculties came into being: in 1853 the School of Natural Science and that of Law and Modern History were created, followed in 1870 by the School of Theology, and in 1873 by the separation of Law and Modern History into separate faculties.

In that year, too, English literature was made one of the four parts of the Pass Degree requirements, and candidates were examined in one of three periods, namely,

1. Selections from Chaucer, and *Piers Plowman*.
2. Four plays of Shakespeare, *Macbeth, Merchant of Venice, Richard II*, and *Hamlet*.
3. Selections from Dryden, with Pope's *Essay on Man*, and the *Satires and Epistles*.[7]

When the School of Modern History was separated from that of Law, the Board of Studies for Modern History proposed that a Professor of English Literature should be attached to their school,

---

[6] V. H. H. Green, *Oxford Common Room*, 1957, p. 171.
[7] C. H. Firth, *The School of English Language and Literature*, 1909, p. 21.

but Stubbs, the Regius Professor, rejected the idea, and when it was put to the Commissioners in 1877, he dissociated himself from the move in no uncertain terms. He declared that he was 'opposed to having a professorship or lectureship in English Literature connected with the Historical School. I think that to have the History School hampered with dilettante teaching, such as the teaching of English Literature, must necessarily do great harm to the School.' He later modified the tone of his remarks, and explained that he did not object to the creation of such a Chair in itself, but to its connection with the History School. The historian of the English constitution had no time for such broader conceptions of history, and expressed the remarkable view that 'there is no special connection between English Literature and Modern History, and the subject might just as well be connected with theology or language'. Stubbs's predecessor in the Regius Chair, Goldwin Smith, told the Commissioners in his evidence that while English literature could only be properly studied in its historical perspective, it should be made a separate study and not connected with that of history. He suggested that there should be two professors of English literature, one literary and the other linguistic. Another witness, R. L. Nettleship, the Balliol philosopher, advocated an Honours School of Modern Literature, to include English, German, French, and other modern languages.[8] A similar proposal was made in Cambridge in the following year, when the Senate agreed to create a 'Board for the supervision of the study of modern and medieval languages in the University'.

Thus the idea of a School of English Studies in Oxford was being mooted before the Commissioners of 1877. There was already in existence one Professorship of English, the Anglo-Saxon Chair held twice by John Earle, from 1849 to 1854, and again between 1876 and 1903. In his evidence to this Commission, Earle maintained that his Chair had a closer connection with philology than with history, and stated that he had 'always recognised the professorship of Anglo-Saxon as being the professorship of the English language'. On this point, however, the

---

[8] *Royal Commission on Oxford and Cambridge, Minutes of Evidence*, 1881, pp. 75, 104, 221, and 227.

historian Goldwin Smith disagreed, and told the Commissioners that he would resist a move to convert the Anglo-Saxon Chair to one of English Philology. The duties of the Professor had been extended during the previous phase of reform in 1858, when Old Low German dialects and the antiquities of northern Europe were included in his scope. At that time the Professor was Joseph Bosworth, who in 1878 was to be the co-founder of the Elrington and Bosworth Chair of Anglo-Saxon in Cambridge, to which W. W. Skeat was appointed.

Earle's first tenure of the Oxford Chair, between 1849 and 1854, was terminated after five years in accordance with the old statutes governing his appointment. This condition, together with clauses forbidding marriage and Fellowship of the Society of Antiquaries, was amended in 1858 when the broader field of Germanic antiquities was added to the Professor's province. The Chair, with its curious restrictions, was originally founded in 1795, almost forty years after Dr. Richard Rawlinson's bequest, and it was therefore a surviving link with a much earlier period of Anglo-Saxon studies in Oxford.[9] The Oxford English School was created not only from the comparatively new development of the study of English literature, but also from Anglo-Saxon interests in a tradition independent of, and in many respects quite alien to, those moral and cultural attitudes I have described in earlier chapters.

The beginnings of Anglo-Saxon scholarship derive from the Reformation, when ancient manuscripts and records were taken together with all other properties from the dissolved and despoiled religious houses. In the general scramble many documents must have perished or been lost, but some were preserved or transcribed, as for example the valuable collection which Archbishop Parker left to Corpus Christi College in Cambridge. An interest in Anglo-Saxon studies was stimulated by the great issues of the age: by the polemical desire to find in the old English Church a prototype of the new Reformed Church, and, in the early seventeenth century, by the urgent political concern to justify the demand for parliamentary and civil liberties by finding precedence for them in the days before 'the Norman yoke' descended

[9] C. H. Firth, op. cit., p. 10.

on the English people.[10] Just before the Civil War, Henry Spelman founded a lectureship in Cambridge, which was then less Stuart in its sympathies than Oxford, to promote the study of 'domestique Antiquities touching our Church and reviving the Saxon tongue'.[11] The first lecturer was Abraham Wheloc, and in 1644 he produced through the Cambridge press an edition of Anglo-Saxon laws, and the first English editions of Bede's *Ecclesiastical History*, both the Latin and the Saxon versions, and of the *Anglo-Saxon Chronicle*, for which he used the manuscript bequeathed by Matthew Parker.

The sentiment for things Anglo-Saxon was widely diffused in the first half of the seventeenth century, and made itself felt in the linguistic consciousness, where a fashion for monosyllabic Saxon 'purity', in reaction to the earlier vogue of rotund Latinisms, contributed towards the complex evolution of a plain prose style. During the Commonwealth more effort was made to study the Anglo-Saxon language itself, and to this end in 1653, after Wheloc's death, the Spelman family transferred the stipend of their lectureship to assist William Somner in Oxford. Somner was preparing the first dictionary of Anglo-Saxon, with the aid of manuscript vocabularies compiled by other scholars; the Oxford University Press printed his *Dictionarium Saxonico-Latino-Anglicum* with type specially purchased in 1656. After the Restoration, Oxford became the centre of Anglo-Saxon studies: Francis Junius and William Marshall, who had worked together while abroad in editing the Caedmonian poems (1655) and the Gospels from the Codex Argentius, were reunited in Oxford in 1676. The famous Junius was the inspiration of young scholars, and though he died soon afterwards in 1678, he bequeathed to the university his transcripts and his printing-type. His friend and colleague Marshall was the Rector of Lincoln College, where he trained one of the greatest Saxonists of the day, George Hickes. Subsequently Hickes compiled the first grammar of Anglo-Saxon in 1689, and was in charge of that monument of collaborative scholarship, the great *Thesaurus*, printed between 1703 and 1705 by the Oxford

[10] C. Hill, *Puritanism and Revolution*, 1958, 'The Norman Yoke', pp. 50–122.
[11] D. C. Douglas, *English Scholars*, 1939, 'The Saxon Past', pp. 60–92.

University Press with the precious Junian type, rescued in 1697 from 'a hole in Dr. Hyde's study'.[12]

Towards the end of the seventeenth century, it was the Queen's College which became the 'nest of Saxonists' in Oxford. In 1679 the college instituted a lectureship in the subject for William Nicholson, whose future career as a bishop and champion of the English Church serves to illustrate the continued link between Anglo-Saxon studies and militant Protestantism. Ten years later, just after the Revolution which sent Stuarts and Popery packing for good, Edmund Gibson came to Queen's, to begin as a Saxonist a career in the Church even more brilliant than that of Nicholson. In the same year of 1689, the college also admitted Edward Thwaites; when he was made 'a preceptor in the Saxon tongue' there in 1698, he had no less than fifteen pupils, and, as he complained to Humfrey Wanley, he needed dictionaries suitable for them. Thus under Thwaites' supervision one of the pupils, Thomas Benson, made a condensed version of Somner's *Dictionarium* in 1701. His other students were also encouraged to further Saxon learning, and with his help Christopher Rawlinson prepared an edition of Alfred's version of Boethius. It was Thwaites who found the Junian type again and restored it to the Oxford University Press, where it was used to print the Boethius in 1698. Another of his pupils was William Elstob, whom Hickes encouraged to prepare a Latin translation of Wulfstan's *Homily* in 1701. Elstob referred to this as 'the first fruits of his labours in the Saxon tongue', while his more ambitious project, an edition of the Saxon laws to include a Latin version by Somner, was planned but not completed before his death in 1715. Elstob also collaborated with his sister Elizabeth in 1709, by providing a Latin translation for her edition of Aelfric's *Homily on St. Gregory's Day*. Nichols tells us that Hickes was Elizabeth Elstob's maternal grandfather, 'a circumstance which may account at least for her proficiency, if not for the origin of her Saxon studies'. 'The justly celebrated Saxon Nymph', as she was quaintly called, endeavoured to popularize Anglo-Saxon studies, and wittily defended her

---

[12] J. Nichols, *Literary Anecdotes of the Eighteenth Century*, 6 vols., 1812, iv. 147. See pp. 112–40 for the account of the Elstobs, and pp. 141–9 for that of Edward Thwaites. See also *Times Literary Supplement*, 28 September 1933, 'The Saxon Nymph'.

abstruse tastes in an age which preferred ladies to remain uncontaminated by learning. In 1715 she published the *Rudiments of Grammar for the English-Saxon Tongue,* for those 'whose Education hath not allowed them an acquaintance with the Grammar of other languages', and in the Preface she also mentioned that Hickes had encouraged her to edit and translate the sermons of Aelfric. In her desire to bring Anglo-Saxon before a wider public, she defended that cardinal principle of continuity which is still implied where the subject is called Old English:

I have chosen rather to use such English as would be both intelligible and best express the Saxon: that as near as possible both the Saxon and the English might be discerned to be of the same kindred and Affinity.

The collection of sermons remained unpublished, probably because she failed to secure material support for her project. Elizabeth Elstob died in 1756, a year after Dr. Richard Rawlinson (who should not be confused with his namesake Christopher) had bequeathed to the university the endowments for its first Professorship of Anglo-Saxon.

It is almost impossible to overestimate the importance and value of this school of Saxonists in Oxford. Remarkable for their close association in a common enterprise, the industrious enthusiasm of these learned men (and of the woman) restored contact with the distant but not discarded past, and passed on to future scholars manuscripts rescued from oblivion, and much of the apparatus for evaluating them. This, too, in an age which often arrogantly dismissed medieval learning as barbarous and uncouth. Single distinctions are perhaps invidious within such a corporate movement, but no one contributed more to the future by his efforts than Humfrey Wanley. Leaving University College in 1695 without a degree, to work as an assistant in the Bodleian Library, he was soon noticed by Hickes for his antiquarian zeal, and in 1699 the older man sent his protégé to search for Saxon manuscripts up and down the country. Eventually in 1708 Wanley received the patronage of Harley, the Earl of Oxford, and thenceforth devoted himself to extending and cataloguing Harley's library of manuscripts. The great catalogue of the

Harleian collection, published in 1759 over thirty years after Wanley's death, laid the foundations for the critical and comparative study of the manuscripts of early English literature.

Anglo-Saxon studies were revolutionized by the new philology of the nineteenth century. The great inspiration to philological scholarship came from the comparative principles laid down in 1818 by Rask, the Danish scholar, and four years later by his more famous German contemporary, Jacob Grimm. Two Englishmen brought the new philology to England: Benjamin Thorpe had studied under Rask, and J. M. Kemble was a pupil of Grimm. It was Kemble who in 1837 attacked Oxford's old-fashioned approach to Anglo-Saxon, and claimed that Grimm's system 'can henceforth alone form the basis of any philosophical study of the Teutonic tongues'. During the next twenty years, until Kemble's death in 1857, almost all the extant Anglo-Saxon poetry was edited by one or other of these two scholars. The new German philological methods came to Oxford in 1868, when the Chair of Comparative Philology was created for Max Müller. There were, moreover, other widely diffused reasons behind the prestige which Anglo-Saxon studies enjoyed in the nineteenth century. Intellectually, the prevalent organic and evolutionary ways of thought fostered a curiosity about the origins of language and culture, and many of the enlightened group who wished to see a School of English Studies in Oxford intended it to include what Professor Earle called,[13] in a significant metaphor, the 'embryology' of the subject. Politically, too, the Victorians tended to regard the Germans as their natural allies, while the French were the traditional enemy: Protestantism and the Queen's marriage and family connections bound the two Saxon nations together. And no less important than this predisposition to recall the common origins of the Teutonic races was the emulation by some Oxford reformers of German academic methods, the professorial system and the concept of a university as an institution for the pursuit of advanced knowledge in all fields.

The political move in Oxford towards the creation of a Professorship of English Literature or a Faculty of English arose there-

13 In a letter to *The Times*, 8 June 1887.

fore from the prolonged controversy between the 'ancients' and 'moderns', between those who wished to preserve the college system of tutorial instruction in the traditional general education of Classics, and those on the other hand who wished to increase the specialisms of new university faculties and professorial scholarship, and to extend the functions of the university beyond the teaching of undergraduates. 'The separation between Jowett and myself', observed Mark Pattison with characteristic bile, 'consists in a difference upon the fundamental question of university politics—viz. Science and Learning v. School Keeping'.[14]

[14] V. H. H. Green, op. cit., p. 260.

VI

JOHN CHURTON COLLINS AND THE
ATTACK ON OXFORD

OXFORD politics often bear a curiously inverted relation to those of the world outside, so that radical principles in university affairs may be quite consistently conservative if referred to the national situation, and vice versa. In our own time, for example, we have heard compulsory Latin defended in Oxford, not as a bastion of privilege, but in order to protect the interests of the less-privileged state schools; and we have seen the election of a Chancellor who represented the Right in national politics, but who in the Oxford contest was the candidate of an anti-oligarchic opposition. It is not wholly the element of the perverse in academic reasoning which brings about these ironic reversals; so strong is the hold of tradition over Oxford minds, even when they are in full revolt against it, and so well-insulated is the parochial world of the university from the currents of change and crisis around it, that ideas and developments in the larger world are often reflected in Oxford as in a distorting mirror. A failure to appreciate the extent to which Oxford is a law unto herself has brought many ardent campaigners and reformers to grief and frustration at her gates, and the attempts to found an English School there proved no exception. The crux of the matter was that the study of English literature had developed in England as the poor man's Classics, as part of a liberal humane education, providing a cultural continuity that otherwise seemed in danger of extinction in the social upheavals of a new industrial democracy; moreover, the moral and cultural potentialities of the subject were being strangled by the rigid examination system in schools and in the new university colleges. In Oxford, however, the movement to establish a new School would inevitably be led by those who thought with Pattison that the function of the university was to advance knowledge at the highest level, not to provide a general and rather elementary education for gentlemen; another Faculty could only be created by reinforcing the professorial authority, at the expense of college interests, which were identified with the teaching of Classics. Such reformers in Oxford were willing enough to undermine the supremacy of Classics, but not to substitute for them a similarly broad cultural education in English literature. It was in particular this philosophy of education as a general grounding in the humanities which moulded English studies in the spirit of Classics, but with which the main reforming party in Oxford had least sympathy. Their arguments for an English School might well have failed to inspire the confidence of interested outsiders, who perhaps found it difficult to understand the wider context of university politics in which the struggle was being fought out.

The first result of the proposals made before the Commissioners in 1877 was the establishment of the Merton Professorship of English Language and Literature in 1885. The Statutes relating to this new Chair gave no more specific indication than did the name itself of any particular field of studies likely to be preferred by the electors. In broad terms, the Professor was to 'lecture and give instruction on the history and criticism of English Language and Literature, and on the works of approved English authors'. Such an open rubric consequently attracted a wide field of candidates, including some of the most brilliant men-of-letters of the day. Edmund Gosse, Edward Dowden, George Saintsbury, A. C. Bradley, and John Churton Collins put forward their names, but the Chair was given to Arthur Sampson Napier, then Professor Extraordinary at the University of Göttingen. Napier was a philologist: his interest in the Germanic languages began while he was studying natural science at Owens College, but he left Manchester and science for Oxford, where he had studied Anglo-Saxon with Professor Earle. His training as a philologist had been completed in Germany, and in Berlin and Göttingen he had acquired the experience as scholar and teacher which persuaded the Oxford electors to appoint him. In his letter of application, Napier undertook to 'advance the cause of the study of English by original work, for which Oxford, with its rich treasures in English Manuscripts, affords most exceptional advantages'. The policy of the electors should really have caused little surprise, but since the duties attached to the Chair had been advertised in such unrestricted terms, the election of another philologist disappointed those who had foreseen an opportunity of bringing a literary man to Oxford: they felt that their cause had been betrayed.

No one was more vehement in his denunciation of the electors than John Churton Collins. His personal involvement as a candidate did not deter him from publishing his views after the appointment, though of course this gave ammunition to his opponents. Nevertheless Collins was not indulging an embittered grudge: his activities during the following years rather reveal his natural gifts as a polemicist and propagandist. Walter Raleigh's impression of him twenty years later was that he had a schoolboy's zest for writing 'clever or scathing "themes" '.[1] Napier's election, however, became the occasion for an intense and unremitting campaign which Collins launched and sustained against Oxford until the English School was finally established. He was determined to bring the issues as he saw them before the nation, and to shame Oxford by the sheer weight of public opinion, though he doubtless overestimated Oxford's sensitivity to the views of the outside world. Nevertheless, the Merton Professorship and the recent establishment in Cambridge of a Tripos in medieval and modern languages, to which English was admitted with a heavy philological bias, seemed to Collins disastrous for the future of English studies, and they precipitated the crisis which had been imminent for some time. During the next seven or eight years, Collins devoted his energies to his large-scale campaign, canvassing the support of influential people, literary or not, and using the columns of the national press to criticize the shortcomings of any academic pronouncement on English literature, to rebuff the arguments by which the subject was denied recognition as an Honours School, and to propound his own ideas of the principles and scope which such a school should possess. If Oxford was the particular focus of his attack, this was because the existing languages Tripos in

[1] *Letters of Sir Walter Raleigh 1879–1922*, ed. Lady Raleigh, 2 vols., 1926, ii, 279.

Cambridge forestalled any immediate hope of a proper English School there, while there was still time to dissuade Oxford from following suit.

Collins was a Balliol man, and from Balliol he drew his educational ideals and his approach to the study of English literature. When he had left Oxford in 1872, with only a humble degree, he had taken with him to the London literary world a passionate attachment to Greek thought and culture and to the ideals of a humane liberal education, such as flourished in Jowett's college. He kept himself in London by coaching for the Civil Service examinations, and by literary journalism; he also edited the plays of Tourneur, the poems of Lord Herbert of Cherbury, and Milton's *Samson Agonistes*. He was a friend of Swinburne, and in 1880 began his long connection with the London Society for the Extension of University Teaching. It seemed to him that English studies should occupy a central place in education, as a means of broadening the cultural awareness of modern life; and his inspiration was a classical one:

It has long been a reproach to us as a nation, that, mainly in consequence of the narrow and obstinate esotericism of the Universities, and partly owing to the unavoidably predominant claims of scientific and technical instruction, we have never risen even to a conception of Education in the sense in which it was anciently understood. Making due allowance for the distinction which must be drawn between the world for which Pericles legislated, and the world in which our busy millions are striving, it still remains that there exists no essential distinction between what men needed then and what men need now. They needed then and they need now to be taught how to live. They need aesthetic culture, that life may not only be brightened, but refined and elevated by sympathetic communion with what is truly beautiful in Art and Literature; they need moral culture, and that on broader lines than when it ran wholly in theological and conventional grooves; they need political culture, instruction, that is to say, in what pertains to their relation to the State, to their duties as citizens; and they need also to be impressed sentimentally by having the presentation in legend and history of heroic and patriotic example brought vividly and attractively before them. To the Greeks instruction of this kind was conveyed easily and delightfully through the study properly directed of the best literature, and particularly of the best poetry; and of instruction of this kind the best literature and the best poetry may still become the means.[2]

If this lofty vision was influenced by the Hellenic mission of Matthew Arnold, it also owed much to the spirit of Jowett's teaching: Balliol was the supreme example of the college system of education based on Classics, by which undergraduates were 'taught how to live'. Not that Collins held any brief for English studies as they were then taught in the schools and new colleges; indeed, as we have seen, he indicted them as 'an utter failure'. But if under the examination system English literature was an easy subject to 'cram', that was not to Collins an argument for refusing to recognize the subject in Oxford; on the contrary, matters could only be improved if the university was willing to organize the subject properly. The potential value of English studies had to be distinguished from the prevailing methods of education, and Collins made his point by drawing a forceful analogy with Classics:

A wretched system of word-mongering and pedantry bears its natural fruits. Two noble Literatures, eminently calculated to attain all the ends of a liberal education, and such as would in the hands of competent teachers be certain to attract and interest the young, are rendered repulsive and unintelligible. A cry arises that the Classics are a failure. . . . A ludicrous coalition—composed partly of malcontents like these, partly of noisy Philistines who never read a line of a Greek or Roman author in their lives, but who 'argue the question on *a priori* grounds;' partly of perplexed schoolmasters, and partly of recalcitrant drudges conscious of the futility of their labours and ready to support anyone who confirms them in their impression—is formed . . . Each in his own way is furnished with unanswerable arguments against their employment as a means of education. It never seems to occur to these persons to inquire whether the fault lies in the Classics or in those who teach them; whether it is the tools which are in fault or the workmen.[3]

In December 1886, a Balliol tutor, R. L. Nettleship, wrote in a similar vein to A. C. Bradley, himself a member of the college and now Professor of English Literature in Liverpool:

[2] J. C. Collins, *The Study of English Literature*, 1891, p. 147.
[3] Ibid., p. 19.

They are beginning to talk again about a modern literature school here. I hope it won't be done in a hurry, but it does seem to me that, if (as seems likely) fewer people are going to learn Greek and Latin, we ought to begin making preparations to supply their place. The discussions about it make me feel how very little the classics owe their present position in education to their being *literature*, for the first thing the ordinary person says is, 'For heaven's sake don't let us murder Shakespeare, etc., by treating them as we treat Aeschylus and Sophocles.[4]

Nettleship had proposed such a School of Modern Literature to the Commissioners in 1877. In the letter to Bradley, he defined the essence of a literary education as handing on 'from generation to generation the finest human thoughts said in the finest way ... the nurture of the soul does require the ideas of other souls'. This emphasis on the cultural process of education, as the distinguishing feature of the Oxford college system, bridged the gulf between Classics and English. Nettleship roundly affirmed that 'it must be humbug to say that a literature in one's own language cannot be made educational'. In the Oxford controversy between the college interests and those of the Faculties and Professors, latent jealousies between Classics and English were obscured. The major issue was with those who wished to introduce more specialisms and direct emphasis from undergraduate teaching towards scholarship and research. Jowett himself had earned but little distinction as a scholar, and Nettleship's letter betrayed a certain impatience with the scholarly virtues, which he referred to as 'the outworks of the subject'. Churton Collins was prepared to go much further, and denounced philology and all it stood for in terms that were almost personally abusive of its practitioners:

As an instrument of culture it ranks—it surely ranks—very low indeed. It certainly contributes nothing to the cultivation of the taste. It as certainly contributes nothing to the education of the emotions. The mind it neither enlarges, stimulates, nor refines. On the contrary, it too often induces or confirms that peculiar woodenness and opacity, that singular coarseness of feeling and purblindness of moral and intellectual vision, which has in all ages been the characteristic of mere philologists,

[4] Quoted by D. G. James, 'The Teaching of English in Universities', *Universities Quarterly*, Vol. 5, No. 3, May 1951, p. 232.

and of which we have appalling illustrations in such a work as Bentley's *Milton*. Nor is this all. Instead of encouraging communion with the nobler manifestations of human energy, with the great deeds of history, or with the masterpieces of art and letters, it tends, as Bacon remarks, to create habits of unintelligent curiosity about trifles. It too often resembles that rustic who, after listening for several hours to Cicero's most brilliant conversation, noticed nothing and remembered nothing but the wart on the great orator's nose.[5]

Far from judging the relative educational merits of English and classical literature, then, Collins sought to unite the two in a common cause, to rescue literature 'from its present degrading vassalage to Philology'. His proposals for an English School in Oxford involved not the dilution of classical teaching and the college system, but its reinforcement and reinvigoration by combining Classics with the study of English literature: 'I have no hesitation in saying that the introduction of English Literature into the curriculum of University studies would, under any other conditions, be as undesirable as under these conditions it would be desirable.' He formulated a scheme for an Honours School of English that would be open only to graduates *in Literis Humanioribus*, and which would be in fact a continuation of their classical studies. This plan was based on his own particular view of the dependence of modern literature on classical traditions; so deep was his reverence for the ancients, that he tracked the English poets 'everywhere in their snow'. But whatever truth there is in his general contention, it was frequently supplemented with violent overstatements of the case:

And what applies to Milton applies in various degrees to innumerable others. The key to the peculiarities of Gray is to be found in Pindar and Horace. The key to the peculiarities of Dryden and Pope is to be found —and to be found only—in the Roman poets. There is much in the very essence of Spenser's poetry, there is much in the very essence of Wordsworth's poetry, which must be absolutely without meaning to readers ignorant of the Platonic Dialogues. Apart from the Greek and Roman classics, the greater portion of Lord Tennyson's best work is, from a critical point of view, unintelligible. The best commentary on Shakespeare is Sophocles, as the best commentary on Burke is Cicero.[6]

[5] J. C. Collins, op. cit., p. 65.　　[6] Ibid., p. 11.

Collins seems as inflexible as his opponents the philologists, and if he was inclined to put English literature in vassalage to the Classics, this was at least partly the result of his polemical attitude. Ideas forged in the heat of controversy are often rigid and extreme. But there was nothing narrow in his proposals for the syllabus of an English School: on the contrary, in his endeavour to avoid 'cramming' and his concern for a broad cultural basis, he produced a scheme so comprehensive that it is doubtful whether any student could cover the ground in three years, still less in the nine months he allotted. Apart from papers on the history of English literature, on its relationship to classical literature, and on the application of ancient critical theories to modern writers, there were to be papers on English history, on the relationship of the French and Italian literatures to English, and, he suggested, students should also be required to submit a thesis on some general literary topic. As an example of the kind of examination question that would require a profounder knowledge of literature than that demanded by simple factual questions about the Christian names of minor poets and the like, he offered the following:

Define the essential characteristics of Romanticism and Classicism, and account for the predominance, at particular periods, of each.

But, not to mention the critical question which is begged here, only the most remarkable student could produce a worthwhile answer to this after less than a year's study, and under such conditions, it would certainly be no less subject to superficial cramming than the kind of questions which Collins, not unjustly, derided.

Collins underestimated the difficulty of converting a literary theory into a practical academic course. It is one matter to illustrate the debt of English literature to the Classics, and therefore to expect a student of English to know something of Greek and Latin literature, but quite another matter to design a school on the basis of such a relationship. The rigid framework inevitably causes other important aspects of the subject to be underrated or totally excluded. Consequently, while granting the French and Italian influences on English literature, Collins was compelled by sheer practical considerations to avoid the issue by asserting that a student would 'pick up' those languages for himself, and that therefore no provisions for teaching them were necessary. He was also quite unjustly impatient of textual problems, and cited, most unfortunately, *Macbeth* as the test case from which to dismiss as merely superfluous all problems of interpolation or corruption.

Ignorance and prejudice could make him as dogmatic as any of his opponents, nowhere more arrogantly than in his assumption that English literature began with the Renaissance. Not only did he pour contempt on Anglo-Saxon and medieval literature as 'the barbarous and semi-barbarous experiments of the infancy of civilisation', he also identified the subject with the philological method of study to which it was then confined: the very confusion against which he had warned others in defending the Classics. The time was yet to come when early English literature would be studied other than philologically, when, for example, W. P. Ker would write his succinct literary assessments of this period.

In discussing Collins's criticisms and proposals, I have taken them as a whole, leaving to one side the fact that they evolved in the course of his vigorous and single-handed conflict with the University of Oxford. Such a programme of the purposes and methods of English studies had never been formulated so thoroughly before, and Collins promoted a new level of awareness even among those who disagreed with him. This is the least that can be said of a polemicist. His practical suggestions for an English course were too ambitious and unbalanced, because what he really wanted was a School of Literature, rather than a School of English. As much as any of his opponents, indeed, he believed that English by itself was insufficient as an educational curriculum, and that it should be studied alongside a cognate subject. His attempt to attach the study of English literature to the Classics, which was the core of his argument, met with little support in Oxford, although it was an idea to be revived by future reformers planning to convert Schools of English or of Classics into Schools of Literature. Classical Moderations were in fact made the preliminary requirement for entrance to the Oxford English School, but in the course itself no attempt was made to ground the study of English literature upon the Classics. Collins failed to appreciate that the initiative and main support for a new School in Oxford would inevitably come not from the college tutors with their faith in the Classics as the only proper study of mankind, but from the party of science and learning, who believed that scholarship and not general education was the true function of the university.

To revert from this consideration of Collins's arguments as a whole, to the sequence of events after Napier's appointment in 1885: Collins fired his first salvoes in May of the following year, when his two-part article, 'An Educational Crisis and how to avert it', appeared in the *Pall Mall Gazette*.[7] The first part of this article, significantly, was devoted entirely to reviewing the state of classical studies, crushed beneath the heavy hand of philology, and threatened with extinction by rumours of a proposed School of Literature in Oxford which would exclude Greek and Latin. The sequel attacked the policy behind Napier's election, and pictured the three philological professors lecturing simultaneously on *Beowulf* to empty benches, while there was no one to lecture on Shakespeare and Milton. Neither did the Cambridge Tripos in Medieval and Modern Languages, founded in 1878, escape his wrath. He traced the evil effects of philological bias in the schools' editions of English literature published by the University Presses, and finally outlined his scheme for studying English and classical literature together, by which the hydra-headed crisis was to be averted.

Collins soon followed up his attack on the evils of pedantry with an even more scathing denunciation of dilettantism. The occasion was his review article in the October issue of the *Quarterly Review* of Edmund Gosse's Clark Lectures, *From Shakespeare to Pope*.[8] 'That such a book as this should have been permitted to go forth into the world with the *imprimatur* of the University of Cambridge, affords matter for very grave reflection', growled Collins, and in the course of twenty pages he pilloried Gosse on every conceivable charge. Detail by detail, Gosse was convicted

---

[7] *Pall Mall Gazette*, 28 and 31 May 1886.
[8] *Quarterly Review*, Vol. 163, pp. 289–329.

not only of inaccuracies in dates and confusion of names, but worse, of not having read several of the works he discussed (for example, Gosse implied that Sidney's *Arcadia* was written in verse), of claiming credit for discovering what were already well-known facts of literary history, and in general of revealing a shocking ignorance of the period in question. Collins destroyed his victim by subjecting the flimsiness of Gosse's dilettante approach to standards that were unexpectedly exacting. Two quotations from this review will show how exaggeratedly vigilant Collins was in order to trip up the hapless Gosse, and how obvious is the relish with which he caught him out:

The following is so exquisitely characteristic, not only of Mr. Gosse himself but of the Dilettanti School generally, that we cannot pass it by. 'Late in the summer, one handsome and gallant young fellow'—Mr. Gosse is speaking of the death of Sidney Godolphin—'riding down the deep-leaved lanes that led from Dartmoor ... met a party of Round-heads, was cut down and killed' (p. 109). Now Sidney Godolphin was killed at the end of January 1642–3 when the lanes were, we apprehend, not deep-leaved; he was, it may be added, not handsome, for Claren-don especially enlarges on the meanness of his person; he was not 'cut down and killed', he was shot dead by a musket ball; he was not meet-ing a party of Roundheads in the lane, he was pursuing them into Chagford.

Neither was Gosse's literary style spared sarcastic analysis:

That excellent man, Mr. Pecksniff, was, we are told, in the habit of using any word that occurred to him as having a fine sound, and rounding a sentence well, without much caring for its meaning, 'and this,' says his biographer, 'he did so boldly and in such an imposing manner, that he would sometimes stagger the wisest people, and make them gasp again.' This is precisely Mr. Gosse's method. About the propriety of his epithets, so long as they sound well, he never troubles himself; sometimes they are so vague as to mean anything, sometimes they have no meaning at all, as often they are inconsistent with each other. What is predicated of a work in one place is directly contradicted in another. Thus (p.34), Drayton's *Barons' Wars* is described as 'serene and lovely poem'; on the very next page we are told that a 'passionate music runs through it'; and on page 75 this same 'serene and lovely poem' is described as 'possessing various brilliant and touching qualities, irregular force, and sudden brilliance of style'.

This merciless drubbing was intended to expose the low standards of literary scholarship permitted in the older universities, lacking a properly-organized School of English. Gosse was merely a scapegoat, and the review was concluded by another twenty pages from Collins advocating once again the joint study of English and classical literature. But the sting of Collins's venomous onslaught was taken, not unnaturally, as an unforgivable personal attack, the more so since the two had previously been on familiar terms, and the article made Collins notorious.

He did not himself come out of the affair unscathed. Tennyson had nursed a grievance against the critic for nearly six years, after Collins had misguidedly but quite sincerely admired the poet by attributing to him the most improbable traces of innumerable other authors, great and small, classical and modern, thus turning the Laureate's work into a fantastic tissue of borrowings and assimilations. And now Tennyson took his revenge by consoling Gosse with his own opinion of the reviewer: 'I think he is a louse upon the locks of literature.'[9] Collins's unfortunate lack of tact also lost him the friendship of Swinburne; defending himself against the charge that he had made a personal attack on Gosse, Collins wrote a further article maintaining that for the purposes of criticism a man and his books were separable:

One of the kindest friends I have ever had has been Mr. Swinburne. But I believe, rightly or wrongly, that Mr. Swinburne's critical opinions are often wild, unsound, and even absurd; that his prose style is still oftener intolerably involved, florid and diffuse; and that he has in consequence exercised a most pernicious influence on contemporary style and on contemporary literature. . . . Now, having last year to review in the *Quarterly* Mr. Symonds' *Shakespeare's Predecessors in the English Drama*, a work which illustrates the mischievous effect of Mr. Swinburne's criticism and style—I wrote as severe an attack on Mr. Swinburne as a critic and prose writer as I could possibly devise. But I have yet to learn that Mr. Swinburne considers me 'no gentleman', or complains of 'mortal wounds given by an estranged', etc. On the contrary

---

[9] C. Tennyson, *Alfred Tennyson*, 1949, p. 490.

the last communication I had from him was a generous eulogy of some trifle I had written, and hearty wishes of success.

What an ironical chance it was that Swinburne had known nothing of this earlier review, and now heard of it for the first time from Collins himself. He quickly disabused his friend of these rather naïve notions of impersonal criticism, and an irreparable breach opened between them, as they proceeded to squabble through the November columns of the *Athenaeum*.[10]

Meanwhile, the real object of Collins's animosity was provoked into a retort, and on 27 October 1886, the *Oxford Magazine* printed an article on 'The Universities and the *Quarterly Review*'. While Gosse and his reputation were surrendered as irretrievable ('we tremble behind our walls of prejudice, but we do not hasten to his succour'), the writer discussed Collins's proposals for the academic study of English literature:

Now English Literature, as a subject of examination, has had its time. Public opinion demanded its insertion in the list of subjects issued by the Commissioners for the Examination of Candidates for Her Majesty's Civil Service. It was found to be, of all subjects, the most convenient to the crammers, the most useless as a test of ability or of knowledge. Nor was the failure due to the incapacity of the Examiners. Great efforts were made to find questions which could test the actual reading by the candidates of 'the masterpieces of our literature' ... until the Reviewer has produced a model Examination Paper we may be pardoned for wishing to preserve our literature from the exploitations of the professional coach.

Collins later did meet this challenge, and drew up a list of questions which set out to test critical ability as well as mere memory, as we have seen. There was of course considerable truth in the charge that the study of English literature had fallen into the hands of the crammers, and Collins would have been the last to deny it, but the *Oxford Magazine* made no attempt to counter his argument that it was precisely because English studies were inadequately organized that the universities should take them in hand.

Collins had already embarked on another project to bring

[10] L. C. Collins, *Life and Memoirs of John Churton Collins*, 1912, p. 114.

pressure to bear upon the universities. In the last months of 1886, he circulated a questionnaire to almost every eminent personage of the day, including the Archbishop of Canterbury and other leading dignitaries of the Church, headmasters of prominent schools, heads of Oxford colleges (including Jowett), statesmen such as Gladstone and John Morley, and distinguished men of letters and of science, including Matthew Arnold, Froude, Pater, Huxley, John Addington Symonds, and Edward Dowden. This impressive galaxy was requested to air its views on the following questions:

1. Was it desirable that the universities should provide systematic instruction in English literature?
2. Was it desirable that a distinction should be made between Philology and Literature, and that the instruction provided should be instruction in Literature as distinguished from instruction in Philology?
3. Was it desirable that the study of English Literature should be indissolubly associated with the study of ancient Classical Literature?

Almost everybody thus circularized furnished Collins with replies, and these were published, some in the *Pall Mall Gazette* during November and December of 1886, and some in the *Quarterly Review* in January of the next year, with a complete reprint in that month in a *Pall Mall Gazette 'Extra'*.[11]

Collins was thus able to marshal a formidable consensus of opinion, not only in favour of the study of English literature generally, but more particularly supporting his own plan for such a School. Some spoke out more emphatically than others: Huxley, for example, maintained that:

the establishment of professorial chairs of philology under the name of literature may be a profit to science, but is really a fraud practised on letters. That a young Englishman may be turned out of our universities 'epopt and perfect', so far as their system takes him, and yet ignorant of the noble literature which has grown up in these islands during the last three centuries, is a fact in the history of the nineteenth century which the twentieth will find hard to believe.

John Addington Symonds even held that English 'ought to enter

11 J. C. Collins, *The Study of English Literature*, 1891, Chapter VI, pp. 97–124.

as a subject into the examination of each student on whom the mark of the university is stamped'. On the other hand, three distinguished Oxford dons, Jowett, Pater, and Merry, the Rector of Lincoln College, were evidently more interested in the future of classical studies than in English literature, and Gladstone himself took a similar view, writing, as a classicist:

Your subject is one worthy of any effort and I sympathize with what I understand to be your views, utterly deploring whatever tends to displace a classical education for those in any way capable of receiving it, and strongly disapproving all efforts in that direction . . . unless English literature be studied in connection with the Greek and Roman classics, its introduction into the Oxford examination system would be injurious to the interests of education.

Matthew Arnold's reply, though consistent with the desire of an Oxford man to preserve classical studies, yet seems curiously out of keeping with his own efforts to introduce modern European thought and literature to an English culture that was in danger of 'provincialism': he should, he said,

be glad to see at the universities not a new school established for modern literature or modern languages, but the great works of English literature taken in conjunction with those of Greek and Latin literature in the final examination for honours in *Literae Humaniores* . . . and I would add no literature except that of our own country to the classical literature taken up for the degree, whether with or without honours, in arts.

It is evident from a study of these opinions that they contain a great variety of emphases and arguments; beneath the surface of conformity with Collins's scheme, the apparent measure of agreement between these leaders of the nation would rapidly diminish if pressed to the further details necessary to bring an English school into existence. But Collins's skill in selecting and manipulating this evidence at the three points of his attack presents to the casual reader an imposing array of consolidated support.

The *Oxford Magazine* was not abashed, but responded with a supercilious answer to the referendum in an article on 'English at the Universities', published on 8 December 1886, and another contribution to the magazine for 19 January 1887 repeated the argument that 'some subjects are fitted for examination and others are not', that philology was necessary to a proper study while the academic study of literature would have 'vulgarising' effect. Otherwise the magazine contented itself with an attitude of snobbish facetiousness, as in the parody of Collins as 'Mr. Random Tearem', which appeared on 4 May 1887:

It is with no small satisfaction that I am able to announce that my recent article on English Literature at the Universities has not been without effect. It is now some months since I rediscovered English Literature and introduced it to the notice of the British public and the Hebdomadal Council. My views have since been corroborated by a consensus of authoritative opinion. I have rescued Literature from the slough into which Pedantry, Dilettantism, and Sciolism have conspired to sink it. The eyes of civilised Europe are fixed upon me, and in a less degree upon the Hebdomadal Council. A literary education is imperatively demanded for the apostles and exponents of literature in Girton and the Colonies, in the provinces and at Newnham, in our public schools and Lady Margaret Hall.

If there were those in Oxford who really wanted to know what educational value there was in English literature, they were not dependent for their enlightenment on the bellicose invectives of Churton Collins. John Morley championed the cause in an address on 'The Study of Literature', delivered to the London Extension Society in February 1887:[12]

Literature consists of all the books—and they are not so many—where moral truth and human passion are touched with a certain largeness, sanity, and attraction of form. My notion of the literary student is one who through books explores the strange voyages of man's moral reason, the impulses of the human heart, the chances and changes that have overtaken human ideals of virtue and happiness, of conduct and manners, and the shifting fortunes of great conceptions of truth and virtues. Poets, dramatists, humorists, satirists, masters of fiction, the great preachers, the character-writers, the maxim-writers, the great political orators—they are all literature in so far as they teach us to

[12] *Aspects of Modern Study, being University Extension Addresses*, 1894: J. Morley, 'The Study of Literature', pp. 57–83.

know man and to know human nature. This is what makes literature, rightly sifted and rightly studied, not the mere elegant trifling that it is so often and so erroneously supposed to be, but a proper instrument for a systematic training of the imagination and sympathies, and of a genial and varied moral sensibility.

Morley was not only preaching to the converted, but lending his public authority to the campaign for a School of English in the ancient universities:

It is because I am possessed, and desire to see others possessed, by that conception of literary study, that I watch with the greatest sympathy and admiration the efforts of those who are striving so hard, and I hope, so successfully, to bring the systematic and methodical study of our own literature, in connection with other literatures, among the subjects for teaching and examination in the Universities of Oxford and Cambridge.

A more direct appeal to Oxford was made by the President of the London Extension Society, Lord Goschen, who was then Chancellor of the Exchequer. In a formal letter to the Vice-Chancellor of the University, dated 15 January 1887 and published in the *University Gazette* during April, he spoke of the need for properly-trained lecturers on English literature for extension classes, and urged that 'every effort should be made to encourage the cultivation of English literature at Oxford by placing it on the same level as other recognised academic studies'. Goschen concluded with the hope

that a system may be discovered which will combine the pursuit of English Literature with the existing study of the Ancient Classics, and which, far from trenching on the domain of the latter, will give them a firmer hold on the English Education of the future, by connecting them with the literature of our own country of which they have furnished the models, and, to a great extent, supply the key.[13]

We are not told whether Churton Collins instigated this move, but since he was then a lecturer of the London Extension Society, and since Goschen's proposal echoes his own schemes so clearly, it is possible that he had some hand in it: certainly it would not

[13] *Oxford University Gazette*, 26 April 1887, p. 381.

have been beyond his capabilities as a publicist to use the medium of Goschen's influence.

Oxford was now mooting a new School of Modern European Languages and Literature. Guided partly by the example of the recent Cambridge Tripos, and partly by their reluctance to establish an English School by itself, the supporters of this proposal also saw in it an opportunity to co-ordinate the facilities already in existence. Provisions for instruction in foreign languages in Oxford, as in Cambridge, were first made by George I, when in 1724 he attached to the Regius Chair of Modern History two language teachers, who were to prepare for the diplomatic service twenty scholars nominated by the Crown. More recently in Oxford, the Statute concerning the Taylor Institution had been passed in 1847, as a result of which there were to be a Professor of Modern Languages and two teachers, of French and of German. Max Müller had succeeded to this Chair in 1854, and under his guidance the Institution expanded to include a teacher of Italian (1856) and one of Spanish (1858), while in 1857 the Taylorian Scholarships were created. The establishment in 1868 of the Chair of Comparative Philology for Max Müller meant that Oxford was once more without a Professor of Modern Languages. A Chair of Celtic was created in 1876, inspired by Matthew Arnold's final lectures as Professor of Poetry in 1867, *On the Study of Celtic Literature*.

In the first proposals for the new Statute of 1887, six languages were to be included: English, German, French, Italian, Spanish, and Celtic. To these the Slavonic group was later added at the insistence of E. A. Freeman, the Regius Professor of History. Students for the School, it was suggested, should offer one language together with its particular parent-tongue, and there were to be papers on the history of both language and literature, with special periods for closer study. In the examination for the degree, 'equal weight' was to be given to literature and language, though, following the traditional English attitude to foreign languages, in awarding Honours no account was to be taken of proficiency in the spoken language.

The preamble to the Statute was submitted to Congregation

on 3 May, when D. B. Monro, the Homeric scholar and Provost of Oriel, introduced it to the House as a proposal in compliance with a memorial signed by the leading Oxford philologists, and with Goschen's request to the Vice-Chancellor. Monro referred to the arguments published by Churton Collins, and to his referendum, to justify the study of literature. But 'there was need of a basis for the aesthetic study to rest upon. He hoped the study of literature would be essentially historical, and founded upon the study of language.' E. A. Freeman gave general approval to the proposed Statute, evidently because it was philologically sound, for he had no patience with the Collins school of thought, and inquired derisively 'what was meant by distinguishing literature from language, if by literature was intended the study of great books, and not mere chatter about Shelley?' Freeman later resumed this theme in print. But two speakers at least, the Warden of Wadham and Mr. Butler of Oriel, expressed their fear that the philological bias of the proposals would preclude a proper literary study such as had been asked for 'from outside'. The preamble, however, was passed by eighty-two votes to twenty-four.[14]

This fear arose from the vagueness of the clauses concerning literature, compared with the more explicit requirements in language. Churton Collins had no doubt that the proposed Statute represented a denial of his demands, and, under the thinly-veiled anonymity of 'A University Extension Lecturer', wrote a letter to *The Times* of 1 June 1887 attacking the projected School. He pointed out that the Statute's understanding of literature was ill-defined, and that in any case there were no Professors of Belles Lettres but only philologists to teach in the school; moreover, there was a danger that such a school would stand in the way of any subsequent establishment of the English School that was really needed.

Neither did Collins rest there: on 2 June, the day after his letter appeared in *The Times*, he began an agitated correspondence with Sadler, the Secretary of the Oxford University Extension Committee, in an attempt at a more direct intervention. He hoped to

[14] *The Times*, 5 May 1887.

meet this Committee, in the capacity of one of their former lecturers, and so to persuade them to make an official protest against the proposed School. Sadler's response, however, was to ask two supporters of the Statute, F. York Powell, the historian and Icelandic scholar, and Arthur Sidgwick, to give written assurances that their scheme would in fact meet the needs of the Extension movement. Both York Powell and Sidgwick were connected with this movement, and taught English for the Oxford Association for the Higher Education of Women, but their presuppositions were not likely to placate Churton Collins. 'The course will indeed include literature earlier than they want to lecture on', replied Sidgwick, 'but a knowledge of the language and the origins of literature will make their lectures all the better.' York Powell wrote at considerable length to explain that it was precisely 'the lack of *good* teachers and writers on Modern Literature' that necessitated such a school as he projected. Literary history would be included, and modern periods would be studied 'by certain picked authors being chosen in a rotation scheme'. '*Mere* Philology' was only a part of the scheme, but 'one that cannot be safely neglected, or good-bye to accuracy'. His assurances that literary interests would be represented were not very convincing: however sincerely it was meant, little confidence would be inspired by his reference to literary criticism as 'what is often called the "*higher criticism*", the discussion of the method, meaning and aims of the various authors taken up (such criticism as Lamb's, for instance)'. Such were the views forwarded by Sadler to Collins, who of course was far from reconciled: 'all you have sent me only confirms me in the conviction that the interests of literature are not secured.' He repeated his request to lay the matter formally before the Oxford Committee, but they were not going to become involved with this firebrand, and at their next meeting they directed Sadler to inform Collins that 'they did not feel it necessary to express an opinion upon the Statute which was still a matter of debate in Congregation and that therefore there was no reason for them to trouble him to meet them in a conference'.[15]

[15] Minutes of the Oxford University Extension Committee, June 1887.

Collins's attempt to intervene thus came to nothing, but, after the summer vacation, as the time approached when Congregation was to hear the reading of the amended Statute, the spirit of controversy arose in Oxford. Freeman's retort to Collins appeared in the October issue of the *Contemporary Review*.[16] His article, entitled simply 'Literature and Language', without particular reference to the proposed School, set out to refute the notion that literature could be studied without philology. Freeman did not seriously attempt to discuss Collins's arguments, but he was obviously riled by the fact and manner of Collins's interference in Oxford affairs, and made polemical capital out of his opponent's rather violent and urgent denunciations:

Men who were doing their own work and following their own studies of others were a little amazed to be suddenly told they were the enemies of this pursuit and that they had committed a 'fraud'—that has been the favourite formula—upon this subject and that.

In the same tone of mock-reasonableness, Freeman moved from defence into attack, insinuating that Collins's campaign was motivated by his own rejection for the Merton Chair:

The truth gradually dawned upon me as I listened to the shouts and as I did my duty as an elector by studying the testimonials and other credentials of the candidates. I had conceived that a mastery of English literature meant a study of the great masterpieces written in the language, in which knowledge and mastery of its minuter philology was at least a counsel of perfection. It did not occur to me that to have written an article or two on some very modern subject was of itself a qualification for a professor of 'English Language and Literature'. The gift of writing such articles well is a gift by no means to be despised; but I should have called it by some other name, possibly by some less lofty name. I might have thought that 'literature' of such a kind, if 'literature' it is to be, was all very well in its own way, perhaps amusing, perhaps even instructive, but that it was not quite of that solid character which we were used to look for in any branch of a University course. Gradually I learned that there were many people of quite another way of thinking. I found that there was something which claimed the name of 'literature' which certainly had nothing to do with solid scholarship of any kind.

16 *Contemporary Review*, October 1887, Vol. 52, pp. 549–66.

Freeman took Collins to task, perhaps not altogether unjustly, for arrogating the term 'Literature' to his own proposed method of study, but his more positive criticism, when it is reached, attains a level of debate no higher than that of the *Oxford Magazine*:

Many people seem to think that any kind of study of which anything can be said, any study which is found pleasing or profitable for anybody, should at once find its place in the University system, and should be made at least an alternative subject for the B.A. examination. ... It is surely allowable that some studies are undesirable because they are not solid enough, and others because they are in a certain sense too solid, that is because they are too purely technical. As subjects for the examination for the first degree, we do not want professional subjects—professional subjects, when fit for the University course at all, ought to come after—and we do not want, we will not say frivolous subjects, but subjects which are merely light, elegant, interesting. As subjects for examination we must have subjects in which it is possible to examine.

Finally, Freeman argues that it is impossible to teach literature, a view which is still not quite extinct, according to presuppositions about the nature of literature:

All things cannot be taught; facts may be taught; but surely the delicacies and elegances of literature cannot be driven into any man: he must learn to appreciate them for himself. ... The crammer cannot teach taste; he cannot hammer into any man so much as an ear for metre and rhythm. ... The crammer can but teach facts; the crammer in literature will have to fall back on the facts of literature, and those facts are, in practice, surely to be largely nothing better than the gossip, the chatter, about literature which is largely taking the place of literature.

There are, however, those with an aptitude for literary studies, just as there are some minds that take more easily to mathematics or languages. What force there is in Freeman's argument that literature cannot be taught certainly challenges by implication the status of English studies as the cornerstone of a general education, a universal subject in place of the old classical training. Nevertheless, Freeman's article does not really take us to the heart of the matter. He endeavours to trap the subject between the Scylla of 'facts' and the Charybdis of 'taste': it is either 'too solid' or 'merely light, elegant, interesting'. These alternatives are false, as well as vague, and it is not easy on Freeman's grounds to distinguish the peculiar merits of those subjects which had found their place in the university system. His fear of the 'crammer' in English studies was real enough, as we have seen, though whether this was something intrinsic to the subject or a result of the grinding examination system was at least open to question. At the other extreme, the prevailing style of 'aesthetic' and impressionistic criticism gave considerable support to Freeman's view of the 'delicacies and elegances of literature' that could not be taught, and the 'matters of taste' that could not be examined. But here again, Freeman's sneer at the 'chatter about Shelley' was in fact equally an argument for establishing sound standards of literary scholarship and criticism, and it is not far removed from the terms of Collins's own attack on Gosse.

If Freeman's arguments were merely polemical, and not really based on any secure or consistent principles, his colleagues in Oxford displayed no greater concern to tackle the real issues of the debate. In October the proposed Modern Languages School found a convinced opponent in Edward Armstrong, a historian of the Queen's College, who published his views in a pamphlet on *The Duty of the University in Relation to Modern Languages*. The point was, according to Armstrong, that the University had no such duty; he scornfully dismissed the scheme as

'the Hundred-Best-Books School', and its first principle is that every book which ought to be read, ought not only to be taught, but be made the medium of Examination. This principle apparently rests on the somewhat *a priori* conviction that nobody will read any book in any language unless he is ultimately to be examined in it.

On 24 October, the day before the amended Statute was to be submitted to Congregation, another pamphlet was issued in Oxford: *An Appeal to the University of Oxford against the proposed Final School of Modern Languages*, by Thomas Case, the Waynflete Professor of Moral Philosophy. His grounds for attacking the Statute were at first confined to the provisions made for the study of English literature, and he adopted an attitude at the other extreme from that of Freeman and Armstrong, being at least partly derived from the Churton Collins school of thought:

An English School will grow up, nourishing our language not from the humanity of the Greeks and Romans, but from the savagery of the Goths and Anglo-Saxons. We are about to reverse the Renaissance.

The Statute certainly did not guarantee a very broad basis upon which to bring English studies into proper focus, and Case showed less prejudice and more reason when he pointed out that

according to the Statute, the student may be ignorant of History, even of the History of England, and yet devote himself to a literature which has throughout, in the practical spirit of England, been essentially an outward expression of the national life.

In the closing paragraphs of his pamphlet, however, Case seems to have abandoned serious discussion in order to pursue an argument more calculated to arouse Oxford conservatism and so to dismiss the question altogether, than to examine possible alternatives to the Statute:

It is impossible not to feel the importance of modern languages and literature. But the question is the proper way to study them. They are already studied to some extent in a proper way. English Literature is largely read in private, and it is open to question whether the individual views and personal feelings, with which one approaches favourite poets, should be shackled by a regular School. Much of the more serious literature of England is studied in *Literae Humaniores* and Modern History.

He then conjured up three powerful spectres: classical studies were threatened, increased specialization would be dangerous, and standards would be debased as a result of popularizing a discipline. 'In this vulgar education Oxford need not compete, because it can be provided by local University Colleges.' The transition he makes from honest discussion to mere bogey-raising suggests that Case was sufficiently cunning to appeal on as many fronts as possible, realizing that both the ardent supporters and the bitter opponents of literary studies could here join their forces to defeat a moderate scheme that satisfied neither party.

The amendments to the Statute were nevertheless approved on 25 October, and on 31 October, the day before the final vote on the School in Congregation, York Powell published a somewhat tame reply to these critics. His pamphlet, *The Proposed Final School of Modern Languages and Literature*, defends the School as a response to 'a real definite demand on the one hand for a scientific study of the Modern Languages, on the other for an historical and critical study of the Literature of those tongues'. Perhaps with Napier in mind (he did not want to go too far to the 'literary' side), he reminded his readers that 'English members of this university have been driven abroad to study their own language and literature in Germany'.

In the discussion of the Statute before Congregation on 1 November, Professor Freeman's voice was again heard in reluctant support of the school. If it were possible, he said, he would gladly resort to 'the sounder educational schemes of his own youth', but the fact was that 'the nineteenth century in which they lived drove them to this', and they were forced to a 'modern' language school in default of a 'Universal' language school. A more heartening view was expressed by Henry Nettleship, brother of the Balliol philosopher and Professor of Latin, who derided the cry of harm to the classics, deplored the consideration of colleges' convenience in organizing university studies, and stated firmly that the basic issue was whether those subjects were worth encouraging. This speech, which would have pleased his mentor Mark Pattison, removed many of the red herrings which had been drawn into the debate. The vote, however, was ninety-two for and ninety-two against, and the Statute was therefore rejected as having failed to secure a majority.[17]

The frustration of this attempt was fortunate for English studies, not only because the provisions for the teaching of literature were inadequate, but also, as Collins had pointed out, because with such a school already in existence the establishment of the English School that was really called for would have been delayed for even longer. This in fact was the case at Cambridge, where English studies had to struggle for many more years before

17 *The Times*, 2 November 1887.

gaining independence from the Tripos of Medieval and Modern Languages. The proposed Statute had failed to satisfy either of the extreme parties, but the consequent stalemate compelled them to clarify their positions. At the next trial of strength, many of the old champions had gone, and with them disappeared much of the obtuse and perverse dialectic which had clouded the issue.

VII

THE FOUNDING OF THE OXFORD
ENGLISH SCHOOL

'THE vote of Congregation on November 1st will probably not be taken by either party as a final settlement of the question.' The opening words of a pamphlet by Henry Nettleship mark the beginning of another phase in the struggle towards a School of English in Oxford. For although the pamphlet was entitled *The Study of Modern European Languages and Literature*, Nettleship gave most of his attention to the claims of English studies. He considered that the debate on the rejected Statute had not honestly faced the real issue: whether such subjects were worthy of academic study. Dismissing many of the eccentric arguments and doubts voiced in Congregation by opponents of a Modern Literature School, he also attempted to assess and reassert the necessity of philology. Nettleship indicated the genuine weakness in Churton Collins's scheme for a joint study of classical and modern literatures: three years were not sufficient for this to be done properly, and in any case 'Horace is the child of his time, and Pope of his. . . . Thorough reading of literature is historical reading.' He refused to accept Collins's view that philology was inimical to literature:

My own belief is that philology can never, from the nature of the case, be hostile to literature, whatever temporary misunderstandings may arise between them. I believe also that philology is a necessary adjunct to the academical study of literature; that the academical study of literature, without philology, is a phantom which will vanish at the dawn of day.

In principle, no doubt, Nettleship was closer to the truth than Collins, who held that never the twain should meet, but there is a certain disingenuousness about Nettleship's failure to recognize the more practical and political factors that provoked Collins.

Exactly what literature was to be studied in an English School? The pabulum of philologists was solidly medieval; linguistic interest did not, except by chance, coincide with literary quality; and on modern literature philologists had little to say that was of interest to literary critics. Moreover, even if the principle were conceded that philology was 'a necessary adjunct' to literary study, was it any more so than history, or philosophy, or rhetoric, or comparative literature? These issues would directly affect the actual organization of an English School and the definition of its scope and flexibility.

Instead of attacking the problem in this practical spirit, Nettleship endeavoured to defend philology in the terms of a familiar and then fashionable educational psychology. Philology offered, he claimed, an astringent mental discipline that would train the mind and provide a balance to the aesthetic appeal of a more purely literary study: 'singleness of intellectual effort is closely connected with, perhaps is only another form of, intensity of emotion'. Apart from the dubious antithesis underlying this argument, the intrinsic necessity of philology still remained to be demonstrated, for doubtless there were other cognate studies capable of fulfilling the same 'stiffening' function. Nettleship's argument is a thinly disguised version of the inveterate suspicion that literary study demands neither knowledge nor thought.

While Nettleship removed many of the old superstitions and prejudices which stood in the way of the establishment of English studies in Oxford, he was no more able than any of his contemporaries in the university to appreciate the nature of the status achieved by English literature in nineteenth-century industrial culture. The demand made upon Oxford to recognize the subject, a demand represented at an official level by Goschen's letter to the Vice-Chancellor, was interpreted, even by sympathizers like Nettleship, not as a request that Oxford adjust herself to the needs of a changing society, which it was, but as an invitation to Oxford to impose her scholastic principles on the outside world. The shortage of good teachers of literature was interpreted in Oxford as a shortage of teachers trained in philology, and many, like Nettleship, sincerely believed that as philology was the only suitably academic approach to literature, this was what the country wanted, even if it was insufficiently enlightened to know it. This restricted attitude becomes apparent in the final paragraphs of Nettleship's pamphlet, where he is not countering Churton Collins nor justifying philology, but addressing a general plea to the university to recognize and encourage English studies, of the kind then represented by the work on the new *Oxford English Dictionary*:

An adequate scheme for a Modern Language school would, no doubt, include the study of all the languages mentioned in the defeated statute. But what the nation most pressingly feels is the need of a school of the English language and literature. Until very lately, the serious study of English has been confined to the circle of a few enthusiasts, who have done much, but might, I dare say, have done more, had their efforts been seconded by a University organization. The national importance of the study has recently been recognized by the Government, more recently still by the University of Cambridge. When the Government thinks it worthwhile (as it most assuredly is) to aid Dr. Murray towards the completion of his great lexicon, will it be said that it is unworthy of the University of Oxford to organize the study of the English language and literature? The country asks for light; we can give light, but we refuse it. . . .

Nettleship was answered by Collins in a letter to the *Academy* in December 1887, entitled, 'Philology *versus* Literature'. Collins cited Richard Bentley's edition of *Paradise Lost* to illustrate his assertion that philologists as a race are generally purblind in moral and intellectual vision, coarse in feeling, presumptuous in ignorance, and worse; after this thunderous contempt, it seems but a minor concession to grant that they are also incapable of responding properly to literature. This is little more than a rhetorical fling, of course, and even Bentley's critical acuteness on Milton may be misguided, but not so readily dismissed as mere folly. This squib added little of significance to the controversy, for Collins had nothing new to say.[1] Once again, however, Collins missed the real issue in Oxford's affairs, that Nettleship, as a disciple of Mark Pattison, was more concerned with advanced

[1] *Academy*, Vol. XXXII, 17 December 1887, pp. 407–8.

scholarship than with popular culture. And certainly, until Walter Raleigh came in 1904, Oxford's contribution to English studies was represented almost entirely by the remarkable number of philological scholars, above all by the work of Murray, Henry Bradley, and Craigie for the *Dictionary*. But this brilliant assembly had little to do with the creation of a school for teaching undergraduates or organizing the training of large numbers of research students.

Meanwhile, in the aftermath of the failure of the Modern Languages Statute, Congregation rejected by ninety-four votes to twenty-five a proposal on 15 November to amalgamate Napier's Merton Professorship with the Anglo-Saxon Chair at the next vacancy, when £300 was to be transferred thence to the Chair of Poetry, itself to be renamed the Professorship of English Literature and Poetry. A similar attempt to even the balance between philology and literature, or between medieval and modern literature, was renewed successfully some years later, when the Statute for a School of English Language and Literature was eventually passed.

It was not until 1891 that another move was made in this direction. In June of that year a memorial signed by 108 members of Congregation was addressed to the Hebdomadal Council, petitioning for an English School. The signatories included the three philological Professors, Earle, Müller, and Napier, as well as D. B. Monro, R. L. Nettleship, Arthur Sidgwick, and F. York Powell, each of whom had already spoken in favour of the subject, together with C. H. Firth, who was eventually to take a leading part in shaping the new school. The memorial read as follows:

The undersigned Members of Congregation desire respectfully to invite the attention of Council to the inadequate provision at present made by the University for the study of English language and literature.

The importance of this study, as a part of the education of Englishmen, is now generally recognised. Increasing stress is laid upon it in the Public Schools of the country, in Government Examinations, and in the Local Examinations of the University itself. The result is an increasing demand for teachers or lecturers competent to handle the subject efficiently.

Apart from these considerations, it would seem to be the plain duty of an English University to give English studies a recognised place in its ordinary curriculum. The undersigned are of opinion that this object can best be attained by the establishment of a Final Honour School of English language and literature.

The establishment of such a School would not involve the University in any serious additional expenditure. There would be no need for the creation of any new Professorship or Readership, and the existence of the School would in this case, as in others, be followed by the rise of a body of competent teachers outside the Professorial staff.

The undersigned venture to hope that Council will not refuse carefully to consider the possibility of thus supplying what appears to be a serious omission in the prescribed course of Oxford studies.[2]

The penultimate paragraph was either ill-considered or an indication that the proposed school was to be heavily philological, for the facilities already in existence did not include any teachers of literature. As events were to show, the 'body of competent teachers outside the Professorial staff' did not 'rise' of its own accord; the colleges were reluctant to elect teachers of literature to fellowships, and the school almost collapsed in its early years as a result of financial instability. This is to anticipate, however. The Hebdomadal Council took six months to consider the memorial, and in December gave its reply:

That the Council do not think it expedient at present to propose a new Honour School in the Final Examination, but are willing to consider any proposals not involving the establishment of a New School.

The door was not quite shut on the hopes of the petitioners, but the wheels of Council, like the mills of an even loftier authority, moved with an infinite gradualness and caution. In March 1892, the Hebdomadal Council appointed a committee 'to consider the present provision in the university for the encouragement of the study of the English language and literature', consisting of the Vice-Chancellor (Henry Boyd), the Provost of the Queen's College (J. R. Magrath), the Principal of St. Edmund Hall (E.

---

[2] This and other documents used in this chapter were collected by C. H. Firth and deposited in the Bodleian Library, Catalogue Reference: Firth b. 36.

Moore), the President of Corpus (T. Fowler), the Dean of Christ Church (F. Paget), Dr. Ince, Mr. Case, Mr. Grose, and Mr. Macan: a group not likely to rush with unseemly haste towards a new school. This committee drew up and circularized a questionnaire to assess the feeling in the university towards several alternatives:

1. Are you in favour of the establishment of a distinct examination in English Language and Literature, to form one of the Honour Schools of the Second Public Examination?

2. If so, would you frame it on the model of the existing schools?

3. What subjects would you include in it, as (a) necessary and (b) optional?

4. What staff of teachers would be required to prepare Candidates for the school?

5. Would you require any particular examination, as, for instance, Classical Honour Moderations, to be passed as a condition preliminary to admission as a Candidate in this school?

6. What is your opinion of the following alternatives?

(i) The introduction or increase of the study of English in existing examinations; and particularly, (a) The introduction of literary subjects as 'Special' subjects or as alternative 'Stated' subjects in the Modern History School. (b) The further introduction of subjects connected with English Language and Literature into (1) Classical Moderations (Pass and Class) and (2) the Final School of *Literae Humaniores.*

(ii) A course of study for graduates, with certificates of (a) competence and (b) excellence.

(iii) The same course of study for graduates, with a class list.

(iv) The establishment of a University Scholarship with the award of certificates of excellence or competence to meritorious unsuccessful Candidates. Should the attainment of such a Scholarship or Certificate count in some way towards the B.A. degree?

(v) A combination of any of the above alternatives.

Despite the deviations and substitutes offered in lieu of an Honour School, this marks a great advance upon the state of things in 1887, when the clash of extreme parties precluded any precise statement of alternatives. Nevertheless, though it was requested that replies to this questionnaire should be forwarded by the end of April, another nineteen months passed before the next move was made. On 5 December 1893, Congregation met to consider the alternatives of an English School or an annual University Scholarship in English: one can imagine that the other suggested alternatives caused a complicated reaction that would confound even the subtlest attempt to assess general opinion.

On the eve of Congregation's decisive meeting, five supporters of the school published a pamphlet pointing out the inadequacies of a mere scholarship such as that suggested in 6(iv) of the questionnaire. Not only was it insufficient to encourage the study of English, but, more dangerously, its failure would be misinterpreted as proof that there was no demand in Oxford for the subject:

A University Scholarship, it seems to us, would not in any appreciable degree meet the want that exists, and would be a serious and probably fatal hindrance in the way of anything better. A Scholarship, with or without a *quasi*-Class-list of unsuccessful candidates, would not bring any one to Oxford, and could hardly be of service to those who are already there.

Men who are desirous of giving a considerable part of their University years to a serious and systematic study of English will continue to go elsewhere. They cannot be expected to prefer a University where work in their chosen subject can only be done in spare hours, or (in the most favourable case) after they have expended the time and labour necessary for a degree.

In this forecast we are surely borne out by the Taylorian Scholarships. It will hardly be maintained that these Scholarships do much for the Study of Modern Languages, either in quantity or quality. The candidates, it is notorious, are largely drawn from the number of those who are of foreign parentage, or have been educated abroad. In the case of a Scholarship given for English even this accidental source of the supply of competitors will be wanting.

But the Scholarship will not only fail, and waste valuable time in failing, but it will block the way for the future. Those who have proposed it are doubtless animated by a sincere wish to encourage a new branch of study, but they are trying an experiment that is only too likely to furnish an effective argument against the reform which they desire. If the Scholarship is as unsuccessful as reason and experience lead us to think it will be, the fact will be plausibly ascribed to the absence of a demand for English teaching. The argument will be fallacious, but the mischief will be done.

(D. B. Monro, Ingram Bywater, C. B. Heberden, A. Robinson, Bartholomew Price).

The debate in Congregation showed how deep was the feeling still that English was not sufficiently exacting as an academic subject: 'a miserably inadequate training, however well taught', as one opponent of the proposed school expressed it. Thomas Fowler, the President of Corpus and a member of the Hebdomadal Council's Committee on the subject, pictured the depressing alternatives: if the school were difficult, there would be no candidates, as had been the costly experience in the Modern Language Tripos at Cambridge, where in eight examinations there had been forty-eight examiners and forty-one candidates. Otherwise, the school would be a 'soft option': 'every idle young man thinks he has a literary taste: so that the School would attract precisely those who need a stricter training'. Even the friends of the school held no great opinion of its intellectual respectability. Grose, another member of the Hebdomadal Council's Committee, assured the House that an English School 'would harmonize, not interfere, with the *Literae Humaniores* School, though it would be really advantageous if it drew off the weaker candidates from that'. An even more magnanimous supporter of the school was the theologian Professor Sanday, who reminded Congregation that 'the women should be considered, and the second and third-rate men who were to become schoolmasters'. Swayed by this torrent of enthusiasm, Congregation approved the establishment of an English School by 110 votes to 70, and the alternative of a Scholarship was therefore abandoned without discussion.[3]

To the Statute then drawn up by the Hebdomadal Council, and submitted to Congregation on 1 May 1894, were added two important amendments on 15 May. The first of these was introduced as a measure 'to secure a competent knowledge of history, the literature, as documentary evidence, supporting and fitting into it', and approved by fifty-three votes to forty. The second

---

[3] *The Times*, 6 December 1893.

amendment, proposed by Professors Case and Napier, was intended 'to secure at least an elementary knowledge of Greek and Latin literature and languages in the new School', was passed by fifty-two votes to thirty-eight.[4] Both amendments correspond to the suggestions made in the Hebdomadal Council's questionnaire that English studies should be linked with the existing School of Modern History and/or Classical Moderations and *Literae Humaniores*. Professor Case, in fact, produced a pamphlet in support of his amendment, *A Plea for Classical Moderations as a Necessary Preliminary to the English School*, which is an avowed summary of the arguments of Churton Collins. 'Consider the moderation of the proposal', he begged, though the arguments he had used in 1887 of 'danger to the Classics', and of the necessity for stiffening a 'soft option', remained implicit on this occasion. A further amendment, proposed by the Hebdomadal Council and approved on 29 May, specified that the school would only admit those who had either obtained Honours in some other Final Honour School, or passed the First Public Examination: this was obviously an important clause, and meant in effect that apart from the women candidates, the English School recruited largely from undergraduates who had passed Classical Moderations.

The Statute in its final form was approved by Congregation on 5 June, and by Convocation on 19 June. At the same time a Statute was passed whereby the Merton Professorship of English Language and Literature was to be amalgamated with the Rawlinsonian Chair of Anglo-Saxon at the next vacancy, the funds thus released to be put towards the establishment of a new Chair of English Literature.[5] This was a modified form of the proposal unsuccessfully introduced in 1887, eventually to be implemented after the death of Professor Earle in 1903.

The Statute created an English School in name: the next problem was to frame the examination requirements which would determine the scope and character of the school. A Board of Studies was set up comprising ten *ex-officio* members and eight to be elected. The latter were to be chosen by the 109 electors of the *Literae Humaniores* Board and the fifty electors of the Modern

4 *The Times*, 16 May 1894. 5 *Oxford University Gazette*, 5 June 1894.

History Board voting together. This Board of Studies was constituted in November 1894, and appointed from its members a
committee to draft the proposed syllabus. The committee con-
sisted of D. B. Monro (Chairman), Professor Napier, Professor
W. P. Ker, F. York Powell, and C. H. Firth.

Without any model to guide them on the comprehensive
structure of such a school, the task of this committee was particularly difficult. Their scheme was drawn up in three parts: set
books, question papers on the history of the language and of the
literature, and two papers on a special subject for those candidates
aiming at a First or Second Class. The arrangement of the papers
was as follows:

1. Old English Texts (*Beowulf* and Sweet's *Anglo-Saxon Reader*).
2. Middle English Texts (*King Horn, Havelok, Laurence Minot, Sir
Gawayne*).
3. Chaucer (selections) and *Piers Plowman* (selections).
4. Shakespeare (about six plays).
5. History of the English Language.
6. History of the English Literature to 1800.
7. Gothic (*Gospel of St. Mark*) and unseen translations from Old and
Middle English.
8. Critical paper.
9. and 10. Special Subjects.

A minority of the committee was in favour of combining papers
(2) and (3) as one, of adding an extra paper on Milton and Dryden,
and of making papers (7) and (8) alternatives for those candidates
who preferred to specialize either in language or in literature.
The principles and problems of this scheme were further explained in a note appended to the report:

The Committee, in drawing up this scheme, have endeavoured to give
equal importance in the necessary work to Language and Literature. It is
not intended, however, that the subjects should be kept distinct on
separate papers. It will be possible for an examiner to ask questions on
literature in the paper on Old English books, and questions on grammar in the paper on Shakespeare.

The Committee have found considerable difficulty in providing for the examination in Literature. They attempted at first to find some way of representing the chief periods, down to 1800 A.D., by means of selected books. It was seen, however, that to do this in any adequate way would require an inordinate number of papers. In the Scheme as given above the Committee have not specified any books later than the beginning of the seventeenth century among the set books. The study of later authors is provided for, partly by the Special Subjects, partly by the two general papers on Literature. It is hoped that these papers may prevent the work of candidates from becoming too much a matter of routine.

The Committee do not propose to draw any strict line between the fields of these two general papers. The Critical paper, besides questions on the history of criticism and of critical commonplaces, might contain, for discussion, passages and quotations illustrative of the history of poetry, or of prose style. It is not necessary that questions of this sort should be excluded from the paper on the History of Literature. On the contrary it is probably desirable that each paper should be made up partly of 'book-work' and partly of 'problems'.

Unfortunately, the modifications made by the Board in their final draft were not necessarily improvements to this sensible outline. Gothic now became obligatory for all candidates, while the criticism paper was embodied in a paper on the history of literature; on the other hand, this left room to increase the number of prescribed texts by including another paper on 'Authors from 1700 to 1832'.

As the committee had pointed out, too many set books would cramp the work of students into a routine, and in 1898 the scheme was altered again to withdraw paper (6) on the history of English literature before 1800, and instead to devote two papers to a general history of English literature, including criticism, before and after 1700. The most important problem was the balance to be maintained between literature and language, and as the committee appreciated, it was necessary to prevent them falling into separate compartments and thus dividing the school into two halves: 'it is not intended ... that the subjects should be kept distinct on separate papers'. Securing a numerical equivalence of four-and-a-half papers on each was not sufficient, and the first

examination papers showed that with the pre-Chaucerian texts
and the paper on the history of language there was no attempt
made to invite a literary approach. The questions on *Beowulf* were
linguistic, grammatical, and historical, and even the romance of
Sir Gawayn and the Green Knight only afforded an opportunity to
display background knowledge of its authorship, its analogues, or
the date of its composition. Passages for comment, contextual,
explanatory, and historical, as well as stylistic, were the favourite
means of testing knowledge of later literature, while emphasis
was generally placed on these texts as documents of literary
history, 'development', and 'influences'. The Shakespeare paper
afforded greater opportunity for critical examination of specific
works, and it must be said that in general the papers on the later
literature were more imaginative and offered wider scope than
those set since 1881 by the university for the special women's
examinations (take for instance a question set in a Shakespeare
paper in 1888: 'Define Tragedy, History, and Comedy, as terms
of dramatic art. Under which of these ought *Macbeth* to be
classed, and for what reasons?')

But there was only one paper which really attempted to combine the linguistic approach with the literary, and that was on
Chaucer and *Piers Plowman*; here six questions were literary, set
by W. P. Ker, and six were philological, set by Napier. This
epitomizes the artificial and mechanical balance between the two
sides of the school, and the failure to reconcile them properly.
The fact was that the principle recommended by the committee
could not be made to work in practice. Not only did the philologists who dominated the new school fail or refuse to conceive
how their study should be adjusted to the wider scope of this
school; there was from the beginning and for many years only one
teacher on the literary side: Ernest de Selincourt (the women, of
course, had their own separate teaching arrangements).

De Selincourt had graduated from University College *in Literis
Humanioribus* in 1894, and, his interest in English studies already
determined, he had set himself to study under Napier and Max
Müller those aspects of the subject which he had not mastered by
his own efforts. After unsuccessfully applying for a lectureship in

English at Glasgow University in 1895, he began in the next year to teach literature for the Oxford English School, and in 1898 University College elected him to a temporary lectureship with the handsome salary of £50 *per annum*.

The reluctance of either the university or the colleges to finance the teachers necessary for the school was partly the fault of those supporters of the school who had wooed the Hebdomadal Council and Congregation with assurances that the venture would not involve a great deal of expenditure. The school was little more than an examination: it could not attract students within the university, though the women, who were now 'placed' in the class-lists, were taught from outside and provided the majority of candidates. Sixty-nine of them took the school between 1897 and 1901, compared with eighteen men. Each of the two university candidates of 1896, in fact, withdrew before the class-list appeared. The following table of candidates for the Honours examination shows the numerical strength of the English School in its first ten years:[6]

1897	4 men 10 women	1902	5 men 11 women
1898	5 men 12 women	1903	5 men 16 women
1899	4 men 15 women	1904	5 men 15 women
1900	3 men 11 women	1905	5 men 13 women
1901	2 men 21 women	1906	5 men 22 women

If the school was to grow, it had to attract the men, but these figures show that it was barely holding its own within the university: the numbers for examination correspond to the intake two years earlier. Matters were saved gradually, by the grant of a Common University Fund Lectureship (an additional £150) to de Selincourt in 1900, by the appointment of Henry Sweet as Reader in Phonetics in 1901, and eventually and certainly by the advent of Walter Raleigh in 1904, as the new Professor of English Literature, the death of Earle having created the vacancy and consequent rearrangement anticipated by the Statute of 1894. That twelve men took the Honours examination in 1907, compared with five in the previous year, shows that Raleigh's arrival

[6] C. H. Firth, *The School of English Language and Literature*, 1909, pp. 35-37.

had an immediate effect on the intake. After a precarious and shadowy existence for these ten years, the Oxford English School now began to grow in strength and to take more definite shape. But this turning point is easier to see in retrospect than it was at the time. Writing to *The Times* in September 1903, C. H. Firth had little room for optimism, and presented a gloomy summary of the state of the school:

With regard to English literature, the position is this. In 1896 the University instituted an examination in the English language and literature, and it had provided excellent teachers of the language, sufficient in number to do the teaching required for the examination and willing to give post-graduates the assistance they need. On the other hand, the University had not provided a similar staff for the teaching of English literature. The study of that subject has been systematically starved by the University, and the colleges have adopted the same policy. The teachers provided by the University are two—the Professor of Poetry, who is only required to give three lectures of an hour each during the year, and a temporary lecturer on English literature at a salary of £150 per annum. At the present moment the University is contemplating the institution of a professor of English literature at the quite inadequate salary of £500 per annum. Our financiers propose at the same time to abolish the existing lectureship, in order either to apply the funds to the amalgamation of the professorship or to devote them to some totally different subject. In reality it is absolutely necessary to retain this lecturer as an assistant to the future professor, and if so large a subject as English literature is to be seriously taught in the University it would be desirable to add a second lecturer.

In these circumstances, any post-graduate who comes to Oxford from America or the Colonies for instruction in English literature will be disappointed. He cannot rely on finding adequate teaching, even if he takes the ordinary examinations; still less is he likely to find the training and help necessary to him to prosecute serious researches in that subject.[7]

[7] *The Times*, 28 September 1903.

VIII

WALTER RALEIGH AND THE YEARS OF
THE ENGLISH FUND

Sir Walter Raleigh (he was knighted in 1911) was born in 1861, and educated at the City of London School, Edinburgh Academy, and University College School, London. From there in 1879 he entered University College itself, where Henry Morley was one of the professors whose classes he attended. Raleigh later recorded his admiration of Morley's unflagging industry, if not of his methods, lecturing 'hour after hour to successive classes in a room half way down the passage, on the left. Even overwork could not deaden his enormous vitality; but I hope that his immediate successor does not lecture so often.'[1] Raleigh took his B.A. in 1881, and went on to King's College, Cambridge: throughout the century, it was not uncommon to pursue a course of studies at one of the London colleges and then to matriculate at Oxford or Cambridge. In 1885 Raleigh was placed at the top of the Second Class in the Cambridge History Tripos, and in the same year he was persuaded by his friend and future brother-in-law, Theodore Beck, to go out to India and take up the duties of Professor of English Literature at the Mohammedan Anglo-Oriental College, Aligarh, of which Beck was the Principal.

Raleigh's career as a Professor of English was thus begun early. His stay in India was curtailed, however, by ill-health, and he was compelled to return to England in April 1887. Nevertheless, as the letters which he wrote from Aligarh show, the experience was invaluable to him as a warning against the abuses to which the academic study of English was then subject. In his reaction to British rule in India, his hatred of the imposition of Victorian

---

[1] *Letters of Sir Walter Raleigh, 1879–1922*, ed. Lady Raleigh, 2 vols., 1926, Preface by D. Nichol Smith, p. vi.

methods of education was second only to his disgust with the attempts to foist Victorian Christianity upon an indigenous culture. For there was to be seen in India, stripped of the modifications and adjustments with which it was trammelled at home, the full rigour of the Victorian belief in examinations and education systems. Raleigh's pupils were being crammed in preparation for successive stages of the 'Calcutta Mill', and there was even less room for a study of literature in its own right than there was in England at that time: 'Calcutta set *books*, not subjects', he protested.[2] Ever afterwards Raleigh carried with him a profound distrust of the examination system, and one of the worst things he could later find to say of Macaulay (whose criticism he disliked intensely) was, after quoting Crabb Robinson's remark, 'he showed a minute knowledge of subjects not introduced by himself', that 'this was the architect of Indian education'.[3]

The years at Aligarh were thus an opportunity to realize even more sharply than would have been possible at home the dangers and inadequacies of the contemporary state of English studies. Back in England, Raleigh had difficulty at first in finding the kind of work he wanted. Cambridge rejected his application for Extension work, and he was contemplating literary journalism, before the Oxford Committee for University Extension finally appointed him as a lecturer on 1 November 1888. During the early months of the following year, he gave a course in the west of England on 'Men of the Renaissance and Reformation'; but in March he was invited to Owens College, Manchester, to deputize for Professor A. W. Ward, who was ill. Raleigh's despondency over the quality of his students, the methods of Ward himself, and the fact-assimilating system within which English studies were conducted, has been illustrated in an earlier chapter:[4] it parallels his reaction to the demands of Indian education. He preferred Extension teaching, in which his own methods found more scope. With feelings of revulsion, however, was mingled a desire for reform, as his views began to crystallize. So, in a letter written to Edmund Gosse in May 1889, he declared:

[2] *Letters*, i. 43.
[3] W. Raleigh, *On Writing and Writers*, ed. G. Gordon, 1926, p. 177.
[4] Chapter IV, pp. 59–60

I am a good deal puzzled—and the question is now a very practical one for me—to get a comfortable or permanent niche in the order of things in general for literary criticism. If it is simply tracing literary cause and effect as history is said to be the tracing of political cause and effect, I do not see why a lover of literature should go on to it any more than I see why a lover of painting should study chemistry.

Thus, in November of this year, when A. C. Bradley became Regius Professor at Glasgow, and the vacant English Chair at Liverpool was offered to Raleigh outside the list of candidates, he was attracted by the opportunity to shape English studies according to his own ideas:

Seriously, I have almost made up my mind to consent, I should have a free hand in my teaching work and no History or Language to bother me—only to get people to love the poets. And a good deal of influence I hope on the general lines of the University.[5]

He did consent, and stayed in Liverpool for ten years. It was a fortunate move, for at Liverpool Raleigh found a stimulating and congenial circle of young professors, some of whom became his lifelong friends. R. A. M. Stevenson (Professor of Fine Arts, and cousin of Robert Louis Stevenson), J. M. Mackay (Professor of History), and John Sampson (Librarian) were three of the closest. In this circle Raleigh also met W. E. Henley, and though he never truly became one of 'Henley's young men', his contact with that bohemian *coterie* and its leader seems to have been reflected in the irreverence and intellectual dandyism of his early book, *Style* (1897). As a young man he cherished the ambition of becoming a man of letters rather than an orthodox academic, and indeed in all his work, even in the more ephemeral, Raleigh's creative bent is evident. Apart from *Style*, however, he produced while at Liverpool some of the books that helped to establish his academic reputation; of these his study of *The English Novel* was the earliest, appearing in 1894, while the publication of his Clark Lectures on *Milton* (1899) drew attention to his gifts as a critic, and his Introduction to Hoby's translation of Castiglione, *The Book of the Courtier* (1899, for Henley's 'Tudor Translations' series), proved his capacity for more exacting scholarship.

[5] *Letters*, i. 130, 141.

Having unsuccessfully applied for the Edinburgh Chair in 1895 (when Henley was also a candidate, and George Saintsbury was elected), in 1900, once more following A. C. Bradley, Raleigh was appointed by the Crown to the Chair of English Language and Literature at Glasgow. During his few years there, he published *Wordsworth* (1903), and wrote some occasional articles for the literary journals, as well as continuing to prepare special Introductions for texts designed for students. But the demands of his lecturing duties were heavy, and almost precluded any other work. When Oxford approached him with the offer of the new Chair of English Literature in March 1904, therefore, the temptation was great. Though the salary would be less than that he was receiving at Glasgow, he would be required to give only forty-two lectures a year, instead of the 160 which, as he told C. H. Firth, he was then delivering. The decision was not easy, however, and at first he refused to leave Glasgow ('The fact is, I am more *needed* here than at Oxford, so far as I can see', was his initial reaction to the proposal), but eventually he changed his mind and accepted, perhaps with an uneasy conscience. 'There is news I don't like telling you', he wrote to D. Nichol Smith, then his assistant. To another correspondent he explained, 'I had to choose whether I would take a chance of being a man of letters, or become a University politician and popular preacher'.[6]

Ironically, Raleigh was destined to become much more of a university politician and rather less of a man of letters than it seemed in 1904. The only books of any consequence which he produced in the ensuing years were his *Shakespeare* for the 'English Men of Letters' series (1907), his edition of *Johnson on Shakespeare* (1908), and *Six Essays on Johnson* (1910), though it is perhaps upon the first and third of these books, rather than upon any of his earlier work, that his literary reputation finally rests. On the other hand, once in Oxford Raleigh soon found himself taking a large share of the responsibility for shaping the English School which before his arrival barely existed except in name. University politician he never was, in the sense that men like Thomas Case were, but the foresight and leadership which the new school

[6] *Letters*, i. 256–60.

needed could not have been found in a mere 'man of letters'. Though he was to speak only once in Congregation, that occasion was a decisive one for the English School.

The means by which Raleigh's election was engineered in Oxford was described in retrospect, by one involved, as an 'innocent conspiracy'.[7] The intermediary was F. C. Gotch, who had known Raleigh at Liverpool, and who had come to Oxford in 1895 as the Waynflete Professor of Physiology. Gotch was also a Fellow of Magdalen College, and no doubt instrumental in securing a fellowship at the same college for Raleigh. The President of Magdalen, T. H. Warren, had been co-opted a member of the English Board in May 1903, and Raleigh's election to a fellowship supplemented his rather modest professorial salary. There were probably other influential allies in Oxford besides Gotch: Raleigh had met both C. H. Firth and York Powell (who died in May 1904) as colleagues lecturing for the Summer Extension Courses in Oxford, while W. P. Ker had supported his candidature at Edinburgh in 1895, and surely A. C. Bradley, then Professor of Poetry, was very much aware of the man who had succeeded him at Liverpool and again at Glasgow.

In his development, Raleigh was scarcely true to type as a professor. From his Liverpool days, he remained more bohemian than most academics; and yet, when he came to Oxford, he would probably have agreed with the most conservative view of the state of English studies in England. On the one hand he did not have that burning zeal for disseminating culture which characterized some teachers of English, and on the other hand he was not a voluminous scholar like Masson, Morley, Ward, or Saintsbury. He was in fact something of a freelance by temperament. The early book, *Style*, was a *jeu d'esprit*, a fling against the usual kind of textbook on grammar and composition which was full of wise saws and modern instances. *Style* is written almost in the burlesque vein, and often bursts into rhetorical flourishes of a not-wholly-serious extravagance:

The world of perception and will, of passion and belief, is an uncaptured virgin, airily deriding from afar the calculated advances and

[7] An obituary tribute to Raleigh by T. H. Warren, *Oxford Magazine*, 1 June 1922, p. 397.

practised modesty of the old bawd Science; turning again to shower a benediction of unexpected caresses on the most cavalier of her wooers, Poetry.[8]

This belongs with those other literary indulgences he permitted to himself, such as were collected after his death by his son Hilary under the title of *Laughter from a Cloud*, and the spirit of which pervades his correspondence. It gives us an inkling of what is meant by those of his contemporaries who paid tribute to his brilliance as a conversationalist. *Style* does not ask to be judged by the serious canons of literary criticism: 'high seriousness' did not appeal to him. He had scholarship, but he did not parade it: his Introduction to *The Book of the Courtier*, his edition of his favourite Hakluyt, or his essay on George Savile, Marquess of Halifax (another editorial introduction) are works embodying patient research and thought. Similarly his little book on Shakespeare, which cost him so much time and care to produce, is after over fifty years still one of the best of countless introductions to the man and his work. It is lively and shrewd, and demonstrates the same qualities of compact lucidity and learning which also characterize W. P. Ker's surveys of medieval literature, though Raleigh's critical sense is more acute. As a piece of criticism, it avoids that occasionally oppressive thoroughness of Bradley's method, by maintaining a balanced and flexible point of view; the brevity lends itself to the *aperçu* rather than to close analysis and speculative interpretation.

Elsewhere, writing of Charles Lamb, Raleigh distinguished between pedantry and scholarship:

Pedantry is the fault not only of:

> 'The bookful blockhead, ignorantly read,
> With loads of learned lumber in his head,'

but of all whose knowledge is a thing apart, imperfectly or not at all related to the scheme of things. . . . The scholar sees all things in a vital relationship, and for him among dead authors there is no dead man. There is thus more of temperament and gift in scholarship than of mere acquisition.[9]

---

[8] *Style* (1897), 3rd edn., 1898, p. 58.   [9] *On Writing and Writers*, p. 94.

In the opening paragraphs of *Shakespeare* he makes a similarly characteristic point:

The indispensable preliminary for judging and enjoying Shakespeare is not knowledge of his history, not even knowledge of his works, but knowledge of his theme, a wide acquaintance with human life and human passion as they are reflected in a sensitive and independent mind.[10]

Raleigh possessed to an eminent degree this flexibility and common sense, this ability to detach himself. We can see it in the above quotations, in his books and judgements, in his reactions to Aligarh and to Owens College, and in his later abandonment of English studies for the more urgent preoccupations of the war. But most of all we shall see it in his contribution to the making of the Oxford English School—his best memorial.

Oxford could not have foreseen how successful and how equal to its needs the first Professor of English Literature was going to be. A great part of that success was achieved only in conjunction with a small group of colleagues: Napier, Firth, and Joseph Wright in particular. Of these, Wright, who had succeeded Max Müller in 1901 as Professor of Comparative Philology, was surely the most remarkable man.[11] Born in Yorkshire in 1855, he worked as a child-hand in a Saltaire mill, and acquired the rudiments of an education in his spare time. The early death of his father left himself and his mother in charge of the younger children, and he supplemented his wages from the mill by teaching other mill-hands reading, writing, and elementary arithmetic. In his twenty-first year, 1876, he used some of his £140 savings to take him to Germany. On his return he obtained a teaching post at Springfield School in Bradford, and while there he matriculated in 1878 in the First Division at the Yorkshire College, Leeds. In April 1879 he moved to Grove School, Wrexham, as a junior master, and after two years moved again to a school in Margate, having been to France to improve his French. He took his Intermediate B.A. at London in 1882, and left England for Germany once again, this

---

[10] W. Raleigh, *Shakespeare*, 1907, p. 3.
[11] E. M. Wright, *Life of Joseph Wright*, 2 vols., 1932, i. 1–139; *Proceedings of the British Academy*, Vol. XVIII, 1932, pp. 423–40 (obituary notice by C. H. Firth).

time to study mathematics at Heidelberg, eking out his savings by whatever teaching and coaching he could find. But once at Heidelberg, he found himself fascinated by the lectures on comparative philology given by Professor Hermann Osthoff, and henceforth devoted himself to that study. In 1885 he gained his Ph.D. with a thesis on 'The Qualitative and Quantitative Changes of the Indo-German Vowel System in Greek', and the following year pursued his studies at Leipzig. He returned to England and then spent the winter of 1887-8 in London, where Max Müller heard of him and brought him to Oxford early in 1888, to lecture on Gothic, Anglo-Saxon, and Old German for the 'Association for the Higher Education of Women'. By Easter he was acting as deputy to A. A. Macdonell, the Lecturer in German at the Taylor Institution. In June 1890 a Lectureship in Teutonic Philology was specially created for him, at the salary of £25 a term. With this new-found financial security in Oxford, he began to publish his Primers through the Clarendon Press, those on Middle and Old High German appearing in 1888, and the Gothic Primer eventually being accepted in 1892. He was appointed deputy to Müller in 1891, and succeeded to the chair after Müller's death ten years later.

Apart from his Primers, Wright's life-work was with English dialects. In 1886 he had begun to work on his native dialect, compiling a *Grammar of the Dialect of Windhill in the West Riding of Yorkshire*, which was completed in 1892 and published by the Dialect Society. Meanwhile, in 1887, W. W. Skeat asked Wright to undertake the editorship of a more ambitious project, the *Dialect Dictionary*. The principal difficulty here was financial: no publishers, not even the Clarendon Press, were prepared to accept the risk, and subscribers had to be found. Wright put his £2,000 savings into the project, and almost single-handed found 920 other subscribers; and in 1896, after an interview with Balfour, he received from the Government £600 and a Civil List pension of £200 per annum. The first instalment of the Dictionary appeared in 1896, the letter Z in February 1905, and the whole work was published collectively in September 1905.[12]

[12] E. M. Wright, op. cit., ii. 349-437.

The *Life of Joseph Wright*, written by his widow (formerly one of his pupils in the 'Oxford Association for the Higher Education of Women', and afterwards through his encouragement a fellow-philologist), is in one sense the last of the great Victorian biographies, in which self-help, industry, and domestic sentiment are the main exemplary themes. To the delight of Oxford society he retained his Yorkshire accent and his racy humour, and a long residence in Oxford did nothing to soften the edges of his dominating character. Most of his administrative energy in Oxford went into the organization of the Modern Languages School, established in 1903, but his grasp of practical affairs, particularly where money was involved, rendered him an invaluable asset to the 'inner party' of the English School in these early years.

Another close associate of Raleigh was the historian Charles Harding Firth.[13] He was a nephew of Mark Firth, the industrialist whose civic bounty gave to Sheffield the foundations of a university, and it was at Firth College that C. H. Firth began his teaching career after graduating from Oxford. He returned to Oxford in 1883, and three years later was elected to a Lectureship at Pembroke College, but he resigned in 1893 as a protest against the College's refusal to establish a Scholarship in history. In 1901 he was made a Research Fellow of All Souls, and in 1904 he succeeded York Powell as Regius Professor of Modern History. Firth was a good friend to literary studies: in 1891 he had himself edited Johnson's *Life of Milton*, and he later lectured for the English School on ballads, of which he was a great collector, Milton, the Restoration, and on the relationship between history and literature. He was more vociferous as a university politician than Napier, Wright, or Raleigh, and did not hesitate to go into print to publicize the needs of historical or literary studies in Oxford: 'I am the last of the pamphleteers', he once proudly claimed. Even the historical outline of the Oxford English School which Firth wrote in 1909 was composed with one eye on the future: he concluded his monograph with a summary of the physical and financial needs of the school. Within the school itself, Firth's main

---

[13] *Proceedings of the British Academy*, Vol. XXII, 1936, pp. 380–400 (obituary notice by Godfrey Davies).

object was the promotion of standards and facilities for research, a task of particular importance now that Oxford was beginning to attract graduate students from other universities, British and American.

Until the post-war years, in fact, a remarkably high proportion of students in the school were engaged in graduate work, and the organization of this kind of training was something quite new in English studies. By 1909, thirty-six students had been examined for the B.Litt.,[14] a degree introduced in 1895. The supervision of these students was mainly undertaken by the Professors, and, after 1908, by the Goldsmith Reader; though occasionally, particularly on the language side, they were assisted by professors from other universities. In those days it was the practice to appoint two supervisors, and it sometimes happened that the same men would supervise and then examine a thesis. The introduction of the philosophy doctorate in English universities in 1917 confused the situation in Oxford, for the general attitude towards post-graduate studies there was in some respects different from that found elsewhere. As Firth maintained, 'the first thing needed is the organisation of proper training for research students; the establishment of degrees to reward research is of secondary importance'. The beginnings of this 'organisation of proper training' in the English School came in 1913 with Dr. Percy Simpson's class in bibliographical methods: by 1925 the school had instituted a preliminary course which B.Litt. students were required to pass after three terms, including bibliography, palaeography, the history of English scholarship, instruction in using the resources of the Bodleian Library, and other subjects necessary for a grounding in the methods and equipment of scholarship. That the B.Litt. has continued to hold its place in Oxford, instead of being superseded by the D.Phil., is explained in the distinction which D. Nichol Smith drew between the two degrees:

The man who gains the B.Litt. is understood to be competent to do research; the man who gains the D.Phil. has researched so successfully as to have made contributions to his subject which deserve to be made known to other scholars.[15]

14 C. H. Firth, *The School of English Language and Literature*, 1909, p. 44.
15 *Fourth Congress of the Universities of the British Empire. Report of Proceedings*, 1931, pp. 83–88, D. N. Smith, 'The Degree of Doctor of Philosophy'.

I have anticipated the sequence of events to refer to this aspect of the English School, because its concern with advanced studies in these years was dependent on the control of the school resting in the hands of a small professorial committee. The colleges showed little interest in the school during the years of its development, and though the Board of Studies was the official legislative body, with a membership of eighteen, it met usually only once a term, and attendance was generally confined to a regular nucleus of the people directly interested in the running of the school. Moreover, the shaping of policy over the specific issues that arose was delegated to *ad hoc* committees, which reported their findings and recommendations for the endorsement of the Board: the names of Napier, Firth, Raleigh, and Wright recur again and again between 1904 and the beginning of the Great War. Thus it is no exaggeration to say that these four men, the last three in particular, determined and controlled the character of the school during those crucial years, reviving it from the nearly stillborn state in which it had been languishing for the first ten years. The advantages are obvious in this state of affairs, for the development of the school along carefully chosen lines.

Raleigh had been in Oxford for barely a year when he proposed a major change in the structure of the undergraduate syllabus, a change which recognized the *de facto* division between 'literature' and 'language' created by the nature of the available teaching, and which therefore abandoned the original principle that literature and language should not be identified with the modern and medieval periods respectively. Raleigh's motion, supported by Napier, was that those who wished to specialize in either literature or language should be allowed to take separate papers, reserving four out of ten papers to be taken by everybody. Those four were:

1. *Beowulf* and other Old English texts.
2. *Sir Gawayn* and other Middle English texts.
3. Chaucer.
4. Shakespeare.

The scheme of papers for those who chose to specialize in literature (the great majority) was proposed as follows:

5. History of the language.
6. ⎫
7. ⎬ History of the literature.
8. ⎭
9. Special Subject paper.
10. Essay.

A Special Subject could be chosen from one of the following:

1. Spenser.
2. Milton.
3. Wordsworth and his contemporaries.

Raleigh and Napier introduced their proposed reforms to the Board on 29 November 1905,

> believing they will facilitate the working of the School and improve the quality of results obtained. The School has to provide for the needs of two classes of students—those who are primarily students of language, and those who are primarily students of literature. Experience has shown that the existing scheme is too rigid, and does not allow sufficient freedom for the development of excellence in either branch of the subject. Some system of bifurcation seems to us the only way to give both classes of students an adequate training in a common school, and within a limited time. With that object in view we wish to reduce the number of obligatory papers which both classes of students alike have to take, and to provide two alternative sets of papers to follow them— one set to be taken by students of language, the other by students of literature.[16]

'Experience has shown that the existing scheme is too rigid': it was not the rigidity of the scheme laid down in 1894 that was at fault, for, as I indicated in the previous chapter, this was in fact intended to provide a flexible combination of the linguistic, critical, and historical interests. The 'rigidity' arose from the failure of the philologists to treat medieval texts as literature (though they were hampered by the lack of suitable editions, and had to lecture in the manner of editors, devoting their attention to translation and commentary), from their neglect of literature after the age of

---

[16] Reports, etc. of the English Board, 1894–1913. Through the kindness of the Keeper of the University Archives, W. A. Pantin, Esq., I have used these and the Minute Book of the Board (1894–1913) throughout this chapter.

Chaucer, and from the inadequate provision of teaching on the literature side. The proposed 'bifurcation' was a recognition of defeat so far as a genuine combination of 'English Language and Literature' was concerned, and 'those who are primarily students of literature' (which itself begs the question) would on these grounds be able to argue that the obligatory papers on Old English (taught by philologists) and the history of the language (dissociated from the literature) were still unjustified impositions on their limited time. On the other hand, whatever principles were sacrificed, the proposed changes would undoubtedly make the school more attractive to students, and at the time this was no mean consideration. Towards the end of his life, Raleigh was to make one final attempt at a policy to reintegrate the two sides of the school.

A committee consisting of Raleigh, Napier, Firth, Wright, and de Selincourt was now set up to consider and report on these proposals. They recommended the reform to the Board of Studies on 1 March 1906, and it was adopted to come into effect in 1908. After this meeting, Raleigh wrote to D. Nichol Smith:

We have bifurcated the English School (leaving for common ground translation from A. S. and M. E.; Chaucer; and Shakespeare). W. P. Ker has pronounced his curse on the separation. Bradley has blessed it. Anyhow, it's done.[17]

Of even greater consequence was the move set on foot almost exactly a year later. On 6 March 1907, Ingram Bywater submitted a resolution to the Board of Studies that 'a Committee of English Studies be appointed to organize lectures and tuition and to negotiate with the colleges on the subject and report to the Board.' Napier, Raleigh, Firth, and Wright once again acted as the committee. Encouraged partly by Raleigh's skill as a lecturer, and partly by the two University Prizes (the Passmore Edwards Scholarship established in 1901,[18] and the Charles Oldham Shakespeare Scholarship in 1907), the number of men in the university who wished to read English was growing; although it

---

[17] *Letters*, ii. 295.

[18] The Passmore Edwards Scholarship was founded to encourage the comparative study of English and Classical literature: it was fitting that Churton Collins should have been chiefly responsible for the negotiations.

had not yet become large enough to induce the colleges to make their own provisions for tuition. But to forestall this eventuality, and so to keep the school well integrated and free from college interests, some scheme was needed to provide a variety of special-ized teaching for undergraduates independently of the colleges. The solution of the 'Committee of English Studies' was a proposal to establish a central 'pool' of teachers who would be supported by fees paid by the colleges on behalf of their students taking ad-vantage of the scheme. Nichol Smith, in a note sent to Mrs. Wright for inclusion in her biography of her husband, relates the origin of what was later to be known as the English Fund:

I remember hearing from Professor Wright that the decision to form the Fund was made in the verandah outside your dining-room, and that the others present were Professor Firth and Professor Raleigh. . . . the scheme was a bold one—Professor Raleigh used to describe it as piratical. Four men—J.W., C.H.F., W.A.R., and A.S.N.—consti-tuted themselves a Committee of English Studies, and were able to secure a majority of votes at the Board. They received fees from students, or rather colleges, or societies, and with the money thus received paid tutors and lecturers. There was considerable opposition but several colleges found it to their interest to fall in with the scheme, and a beginning was made.[19]

The Committee of English Studies, in fact, two months after its constitution, submitted to the Board on 10 May the draft of a letter which it was proposed to send round the colleges. The letter was approved as follows:

Dear Sir,

The increase in the number of candidates for the English School and the diversity of subjects which that School prescribes for study have made it necessary, in the opinion of the teachers concerned, to organize the teaching with a view to supplying adequate tuition, in both lan-guage and literature, for all students. The English Board has therefore appointed a Committee, to arrange the present teaching more systematic-ally, and to endeavour to provide the additional instruction which is needed.

The Committee, if it receives support from a sufficient number of

[19] E. M. Wright, op. cit., ii. 490.

Colleges, is prepared to guarantee adequate teaching and supervision for all candidates taking the School, upon payment of a fixed terminal fee for each candidate.

The fee it proposes to ask is five guineas (or five pounds free of Income Tax) for each student. In return for this fee it would undertake to provide all the lectures, classes, and private tuition which are necessary for the School. With regard to supervision it is proposed that one of the English Tutors recommended by the Committee shall be selected by the College concerned to supervise the whole of the candidate's work, and to report terminally as to his progress and his attendance at lectures. The Tutor selected will make the necessary arrangements with other lecturers and teachers for the various parts of the work, and will be responsible to the College for the whole.

It is our hope that your College will give its support to the Committee in their effort to carry out this scheme. The students taking English are scattered in many Colleges; in no College, for many years to come, are they likely to be numerous. The subjects of study included within the range of the School are very various; and the teachers are few. It is only by co-operation and system that the needs of the student can be adequately supplied.

This letter met with a favourable response from most of the colleges, and the scheme was set in motion. About a year afterwards, however, at its meeting of 13 March 1908, the Board of Studies suddenly realized, with some alarm, that it had no statutory authority to handle financial arrangements; and so during the following term a draft Statute, authorizing the Board to collect and assign fees under the official name of the English Fund, was drawn up and submitted to the Hebdomadal Council to be put before Congregation. While the proposed Statute was undergoing the usual course of amendments between Council and the Board of Studies, in Michaelmas Term 1908, de Selincourt left Oxford to take the English Chair at Birmingham.

De Selincourt's departure was a serious blow to the English School. Before the advent of Raleigh, he had borne almost the whole weight of the literature teaching for the school, and even after 1904 his duties were not appreciably diminished. As a teacher, we are told, he was exacting and even severe. Helen Darbishire, a former pupil of his in Oxford, remembered humbly that 'he seldom praised', and gave an alarming example of the thoroughness of his methods at Birmingham: 'he required all his students to read aloud to him; if they failed to pass the test, they were sent on to a course of speech training'. De Selincourt's application for the Birmingham Chair, vacated by Churton Collins's suicide, was no doubt precipitated by his failure to obtain the Goldsmith Readership, established earlier in 1908. He was then passed over in favour of David Nichol Smith, since 1904 the Professor of English at Armstrong College, Newcastle, but formerly Raleigh's assistant at Glasgow, where Raleigh first recognized in Nichol Smith's powers of scholarship a valuable complement to his own disposition. So Nichol Smith was brought to Oxford to become Raleigh's lieutenant in directing the growing school. Not that de Selincourt's disappointment estranged him from Oxford or the English School: he always regarded it as the best preparation for research and a training in the methods of scholarship, and in 1911 he sent to the school one of his Birmingham pupils, F. P. Wilson, as a student for the B.Litt. The year 1913 was a vintage one for the Charles Oldham Shakespeare Scholarship, and for English studies, when F. P. Wilson was awarded the Scholarship and M. R. Ridley was placed *Proxime Accessit*. De Selincourt himself returned to Oxford in 1928 as Professor of Poetry.

His sudden loss in 1908, however, threatened the stability of the school, and particularly of the projected English Fund. For although Nichol Smith now held the new Readership, and George Gordon had been elected to a Prize Fellowship at Magdalen in 1907, largely through Raleigh's influence, and although R. J. E. Tiddy, a Fellow of Trinity College, was converting himself from a Classics don to an English tutor, these men were new and not established in the confidence of the colleges. The very fact that de Selincourt had had charge of so many pupils meant that colleges which had formerly sent their men to him might now find teachers outside the group organized by the Committee of English Studies. Such an eventuality would have entailed financial disaster and the collapse of the English Fund then in the process of securing statutory recognition.

In this emergency Raleigh wrote to the colleges concerned offering them the following tutors within the scheme: in language, A. O. Belfour (assistant to Napier), and in literature, R. J. E. Tiddy, G. S. Gordon, and H. F. B. Brett-Smith. Raleigh's distrust of the colleges and consequent anger at the jeopardy in which the school suddenly found itself is revealed in a letter written to Firth on 8 December:

> I have drafted a letter to the Colleges about Tuition, saying only what we have agreed. You shall have a proof. Wright thinks it pressing, because they may be moved to make other arrangements in default of information from us.
>
> I have approached them in humble wise, asking what they are going to do, and suggesting that if they have no other plan, our men are to hand, and efficient.
>
> I feel as if I were on the high road to serious politics, which I take to be a kind of revenge for unnecessary trouble and indignity. The material for making me an anarchist is slowly accumulating. If the English School is smashed by a stampede of the Colleges I shan't write anything at all for Oxford readers, but I shall feel sorely tempted to try something outside. As it is, I should welcome a Commission. Meantime, I try to avoid one.[20]

There was no stampede and the co-operation of the colleges was secured. But another exigency to be met at this time was the expiration at the end of the academic year of the grants from the Common University Fund. Firth drafted a letter to the Delegates requesting a renewal of these grants, and proposing in place of de Selincourt's Lectureship the creation of a Readership in Language, for which an additional £150 per annum was requested from the Common University Fund. Firth's memorandum is worth full quotation for its detailed stock-taking of the situation of the school between de Selincourt's departure and the coming of the English Fund Statute:

> In the *Summary of the more pressing Needs of the University* issued on behalf of the Chancellor's Fund, it is stated that the appointment of two permanent Readers to assist the Professors of English is greatly to be

[20] *Letters*, ii. 339.

desired. The English Board itself, in the statement of its needs made in 1902, asked for two Readerships, one in the Language, the other in the Literature, as necessary for the complete equipment of the School. Since that date the number of undergraduates reading for the School has more than doubled, and the number of men reading for the degree of B.Litt. in this subject has also considerably increased. Thanks to the liberality of the Goldsmiths' Company the desired Readership in English Literature has just been founded, and we now ask for the establishment of the Readership in the Language, which is necessary to supplement the higher teaching already given in that branch of the subject and to provide for the supervision of advanced studies in it.

The expiration in Trinity Term of the Lectureship in English Literature, at present held by Dr. E. de Selincourt, will place £150 a year at the disposal of the Common University Fund. The Committee for English Studies ventures to suggest that the Delegates should devote this sum to the provision of the proposed Readership in the English Language, and add a further grant of £150 a year to make the salary of the post £300. The Committee will be able to add something to this sum from the fees at its disposal, as it has done in the case of the Goldsmith Readership. It can promise £150 a year at once, and hopes to raise that amount to £200 if the numbers of the School continue to increase.

Two other grants made by the Common University Fund towards the teaching of English will expire during the present year. (1) The grant of £200 a year towards the salary of the Professor of English Literature expires on 13 June 1909. It is desirable to continue this grant, since it is required to make up the salary of the Professor to the amount promised when he was appointed. (2) The grant of £100 a year to the Professor of Anglo-Saxon for assistance in the elementary work, and the need for such help will not be obviated by the appointment of a Reader to take part of the higher work. There is also a reason for continuing to provide assistance in the teaching of the Language which does not exist in the case of the Literature. At the present moment it is possible to obtain in Oxford temporary help in the teaching of English literature, either in the form of tuition or lectures on particular subjects, from persons not habitually employed in teaching for the School. But persons qualified to give similar assistance in the Language-work are not so easy to find here. It is therefore hoped that the Delegates will continue this grant for the present.

The three expiring grants amount together to £450 a year; the additional £150 asked for will bring the total expenditure of the C.U.F. on this subject to £600 a year.

The Readership in English Language was not created, but the other grants were renewed. The rise in numbers referred to by Firth is shown by the following table of students taking the school:[21]

1904: 5 men 15 women	1907: 12 men 17 women
1905: 5 men 13 women	1908: 12 men 17 women
1906: 5 men 22 women	1909: 13 men 19 women

In 1909 there were altogether forty-nine men and fifty-six women reading for the school. This increase was due not only to the growing effect of Raleigh's personal magnetism, but also to the 'bifurcation' of the examination which took effect in 1908, and to the new variety of teaching and special classes made possible by the centralized system, particularly on the literature side, where the demand was heavier. Apart from tutors in colleges, namely Tiddy and Gordon, the school was able to offer the lectures of the Professors and of the Goldsmith Reader, and also occasionally of teachers from other faculties, such as Firth, Sidgwick, and W. H. Hadow. There were seminars, and a special Essay Class (Raleigh expected his students to be able to write as well as read), together with the occasional services of B.Litt. students lecturing and tutoring in their own fields of study. Moreover, there were often students from other faculties wishing to attend lectures in the English School.

This was the situation when the Statute regularizing the English Fund was laid before Congregation on 23 November 1909. Its principles were, briefly, that while the Board of Studies reserved the right to appoint lecturers and to draw up lecture-lists, the colleges could choose between the appointed tutors; and, to allay the suspicions of the colleges towards professorial power, that the Board of Studies was to receive all fees and to pay them into the University Chest, 'to be used for the provision of additional lectures'. The Committee of English Studies which had been in control since March 1907 was to be dissolved as such,

[21] C. H. Firth, op. cit., pp. 37–38.

and neither the two Professors nor the Goldsmith Reader were to receive any remuneration from the Fund for their lectures. A later arrangement had to be made with the 'Association for the Higher Education of Women', whereby their women tutors became eligible for recognition by the Board. Before the debate in Congregation, Raleigh was still suspicious that college prejudice would bring the scheme to nothing, and he wrote to Firth:

I don't know if we shall get the Statute, but Bank Holiday on Hampstead Heath is something to look forward to in Congregation. The absurd thing is they pay you to shelve you. So it's all right either way, but I'm getting elderly, and should be glad to know whether I'm a teacher or not so as to order my life according.[22]

In the event, the Statute was passed by 117 votes to 65, a majority due not least to an earnest speech made by Raleigh: this was the only occasion on which he spoke in Congregation.

The English Fund Statute was in being until 1926, when the school had become so large that it was no longer considered to need special treatment, and was made to fall into line with the other schools. But it is doubtful whether English studies could have grown and flourished at all without this centralized administration and the scope which it gave to Raleigh to create the school as he wanted it.

Though the familiar Committee of English Studies had gone, it was in name only. On 27 May 1910, a Standing Committee was appointed by the Board to administer the Fund, comprising the 'old firm' of Napier, Firth, Raleigh, and Wright, to whom were added D. Nichol Smith and R. J. E. Tiddy, the latter having succeeded in 1910 to de Selincourt's Common University Fund Lectureship. However, the troubles were not over yet: it proved a difficult task to persuade the Curators of the University Chest to relinquish their hold on the sums entrusted to their keeping by the Fund. As Firth had written in concluding his brief history of the English School, a local habitation was still needed, comparable to the Taylor Institution, with lecture-rooms, class-rooms, and a library. But the Curators were reluctant to interpret this need as

[22] *Letters*, ii. 346.

lying within the scope of the Statute, which referred only to 'the provision of additional lectures'. Their hand was eventually forced by application to the Hebdomadal Council, and, as we shall see, the English Library was consequently formed in 1914. In a letter to Joseph Wright, Raleigh gave poetic vent to his frustration at yet another instance of college influence hampering university interests:[23]

> There were Twenty College Bursars,
>   And they did think it best
> To garotte the University
>   And sit upon its chest.
>
> The Secretary to the chest
>   His life was full of care
> When he heard their quiet whisperings
>   And saw them sitting there.
>
> 'Here be twenty learned warriors,
>   And I', says he, 'am one;
> I dare not pay a penny
>   For anything that's done.
>
> 'Be it known to you, O people
>   Who desire to write and read,
> I will not pay a penny
>   For anything you need!
>
> 'Betake you to the Bursars
>   And crook the humble knee,
> For they are rich and mighty,
>   And they are bold and free.
>
> 'The bed-rid University
>   Can never grant you grace,
> For the Twenty College Bursars
>   Are the Masters of this place!'

Though the establishment of the English Fund was the main preoccupation of the Board between 1907 and 1910, it found time

23 E. M. Wright, op. cit., ii. 491.

to shape a policy in other directions. On 13 March 1908, a preliminary examination was mooted, and a committee set up to consider the prospect. In June, however, it recommended that any such action should be delayed for the present. The proposal was renewed in October 1910, and a second committee was constituted, but the time was evidently not ripe for such an innovation, and the committee was discharged in February 1912. It was still the rule for members of the university to take the English School either as a second Final School or after Classical Moderations.

In October 1909 the Board of Studies gained control of English Literature in the Pass School, separating the subject from the Pass Group to which it had previously belonged, and reorganizing it so that Pass Degree students taking English could attend relevant lectures and classes within the scope of the Fund.

The problem of balancing 'language' and 'literature' came to the fore again in this month, when Napier, Firth, Raleigh, Wright, and Nichol Smith were constituted as a committee 'to consider the whole question of the standard required from Candidates in the Final Honour School for the various classes'. Since the bifurcation of the examination, which had taken effect for the first time in the previous term, the original principle of giving equal weight to literature and language could no longer be operated quite so simply. The committee made its report in December, and its recommendations to the examiners were as follows:

1. Every candidate shall be required to translate competently and well from Old and Middle English, and to possess a good knowledge of the grammar of Old and Middle English, and of the general history of the language.

2. Every candidate shall be required to show a good knowledge of the set plays of Shakespeare, of the set poems of Chaucer, and of the general history of English Literature.

3. No candidate shall be placed in the First Class of the School if he obtains less than half marks in the necessary papers in either Language or Literature.

4. No candidate shall obtain Honours in the School if he obtains less than a third of the marks in the necessary papers in either Language or Literature.

These requirements immediately proved too rigid, particularly in the case of candidates who reached a First Class standard in their literature papers but failed to gain the necessary half marks in language. In the next Final Examination, out of the twenty-one men who took the School, three such candidates were in this position, while the only two candidates who secured more than half marks on their language papers did not attain a First Class standard in literature. Indeed, two of these with First Class marks in literature failed to gain the necessary third of the language marks, and so could not even qualify for Honours.

W. Macneile Dixon, Raleigh's successor at Glasgow, who was examining for the school in this year, with Raleigh, Wright, and A. O. Belfour, pointed out the anomalies of the situation in a letter to the Board appended to the examiners' report:

> The class attained by many of the candidates is determined by their performances on the three Language papers rather than by their performances in the major part of the examination.
>
> A superior candidate in Literature can and does obtain a lower class in the final lists than an inferior candidate, who does well or moderately well in Language.
>
> Furthermore, the oral examination is deprived of a great part of the weight which would otherwise attach to it, since it seems useless to subject a candidate to further tests in Literature whose class in the examination is already irrevocably determined by the place he has attained in the three Language papers.

In the Board's discussion of this report, on 9 December 1910, Raleigh proposed alternative recommendations which were so flexible as to err on the side of vagueness, but he withdrew them in favour of a more precise modification of the original scheme. It was agreed that 'should' was to be substituted throughout for 'shall', thus making the recommendations permissive rather than obligatory, and that candidates of a First Class standard on either side of the examination should not gain that class if they fell 'below the standard of a Third Class' on the other side. This was much more generous than the stipulation of half the possible marks, and destroyed the vestiges of an artificial equivalence be-

tween language and literature. The fourth of the original recommendations was rescinded altogether.

In February 1911 Raleigh became Chairman of the Board of
Studies in place of Napier. A year later, there appears in the
minutes of the Board's meeting on 15 March 1912 the first and
only reference to Henry Sweet, who had unobtrusively held his
Readership in Phonetics since 1901, but apart from providing in
his *Anglo-Saxon Reader* (first edition 1876) the textbook for the
Old English paper, he had had little or nothing to do with the
making of the English School:

The lecture list of Easter Term was considered. It was agreed that the
Reader in Phonetics should be asked either to change the subject of his
lecture on Ugrian Phonetics or to remove it from the list, as in the
opinion of the Board the subject did not fall within the scope of the list.

There is just a touch of pathos in the solitary reference: Sweet died
on 30 April, barely two months later, and the Board decided not
to re-establish the Readership.

The end of Sweet's career in Oxford epitomized the whole of
his dealings with his university, which make rather melancholy
reading. Sweet had already studied at Heidelberg before coming
to Balliol, and whilst an undergraduate he published an edition of
the Alfredian version of *Cura Pastoralis*: perhaps his energies spent
in this direction explain the Fourth Class degree which he took in
1873. In 1885 he was an unsuccessful candidate for the new
Merton Professorship, and again in 1901 he applied for the Chair
of Comparative Philology, to which Joseph Wright was appointed. In 1898 he had been appointed as a lecturer in the
English language at Liverpool, but he changed his mind before
taking up his duties, and instead secured the post for Henry Cecil
Wyld, who was at the time studying for a B.Litt. under Sweet's
supervision, and who in 1904 became the first Baines Professor of
English Language and Philology at Liverpool. Sweet's Readership
in Phonetics in 1901 was something of a consolation prize, and his
natural ill-humour was only intensified by academic obscurity:
even his name seems an ironic trick of fortune. It was indeed a
shameful but not an isolated instance of Oxford's tardiness in

recognizing the scholar of international repute in one of her own sons. He has gained a popular, if vicarious, fame as the original of Bernard Shaw's 'Professor Higgins'.

The new 'literary science' of bibliography, which revolutionized the methods of editing Shakespeare and other Elizabethan printed texts, was introduced to Oxford in 1913, when Dr. Percy Simpson inaugurated a class for research students in bibliographical method and the principles of textual criticism. Associated with the work of A. W. Pollard, W. W. Greg, and R. B. McKerrow, the 'new bibliography' was developed during the first decade of the century. It established more astringent rules of editorial procedure, and made astounding claims for accuracy in textual reconstruction, based on a knowledge of printing methods of the sixteenth and seventeenth centuries. By inferring the course of transmission between author and surviving text, an editor could determine the authority of his text, and base his judgements on observable data and not merely on subjective or aesthetic preferences. The consequences of these new principles, once accepted, reached beyond textual study itself to refute the semi-biographical and interpretative criticism based on the assumptions of Sir Sidney Lee, J. M. Robertson, and other 'disintegrators'. Pollard's *Shakespeare's Folios and Quartos* (1909) discovered the distinction between 'good' and 'bad' Quartos, and affirmed the authority of the First Folio, while Greg's uncompromising reviews, apart from his own editorial work on Henslowe, helped to publicize the revolution.[24] Churton Collins, for instance, was made to swallow the kind of medicine which he had previously dispensed to others, when Greg reviewed his edition of Greene's plays and poems in the first number of the *Modern Language Review*:

It is high time that it should be understood that so long as we entrust our old authors to arm-chair editors who are content with second-hand knowledge of textual sources, so long will English scholarship in England afford undesirable amusement to the learned world.[25]

24 *The Bibliographical Society, 1892–1942. Studies in Retrospect*, 1945, pp. 76–135, F. P. Wilson, 'Shakespeare and the New Bibliography'. Also F. P. Wilson's obituary notice of W. W. Greg in *Proceedings of the British Academy*, Vol. XLV, 1959, pp. 307–34.
25 *Modern Language Review*, Vol. I, 1905–6, p. 246.

The last event of importance in the history of the school before
the war was the foundation of the English Library in July 1914,
made possible by an endowment from the English Fund. Dr.
Percy Simpson was the first librarian: in this year he also became
a lecturer, in place of George Gordon, who had been appointed
Professor at Leeds. He later contributed the following recollection
of the early days of the Library to Mrs. Wright's biography of
her husband:

The original idea of an English Library came from Sir Walter Raleigh.
At Liverpool he had rooms which he could use for classes and which
served as a centre for the business activities of the School. So the idea
sprang from him to get a set of rooms and place a Library in them. The
first books were placed on the shelves in July 1914, and Mr. Brett-
Smith and I were put in charge of them. I remember vividly the keen
interest which Professor Wright took in the movement and the very
practical help he gave us. The first books placed on the shelves were 213
volumes of their own publications presented by the Delegates of the
Clarendon Press, and 129 volumes, the gift of Professor Wright: these
last included sets of the Percy and Spenser Societies' publications—both
out of print, and very valuable—and Arber's *Garner*, and the Professor's own *Dialect Dictionary*. In those hard times of the war we had
only slender grants of £20 or £25 to buy new books; and from time
to time Professor Wright would hand over to me some book he had
just acquired, such as Cooper's *Thesaurus*, 1578; and he also gave
24 volumes of the Scottish Text Society's publications.[26]

Wright was also responsible for the idea of a special English course
for foreigners, inaugurated in 1913. But the war brought this
enterprise to an end, as it immobilized most aspects of university
life. Napier died in May 1916, more or less unsung, for he gained
no obituary in the *Proceedings* of the British Academy, of which he
was a Fellow, nor a place in the *Dictionary of National Biography*.
A tribute appeared in the *Oxford Magazine* from one who had
known him since his undergraduate days, granting that Napier
'cared no more than Darwin did for any literature later than
Chaucer', and reviving with more loyalty than truth the forgotten controversy surrounding his election in 1885—though on
these occasions no man is on his oath:

[26] E. M. Wright, op. cit., ii. 492.

He was the right man for the time; for the English School was very open to capture by the indolent and vague amateur: and he laid its foundations once for all on severe lines.

In fact Napier, who was rather a shy man, allowed Raleigh, Firth, and Nichol Smith to take the initiative in planning the school, and confined himself to his own special interests. He lectured for the school on the history of the English language, but he was first and foremost a textual scholar of international eminence in the field of Early English. It was not until 1921 that Oxford heard a full and generous tribute to Napier, and this was paid by his successor H. C. K. Wyld in his Inaugural Lecture. After Napier's death, Wright organized a special fund to secure his library for the English School, and within a fortnight subscriptions had raised the necessary sum to add the 'Napier Memorial Library' to the English Library. The two Chairs which had been united under Napier were now separated once again, and while the Merton Professorship remained vacant until after the war, W. J. Craigie, a co-editor of the *New English Dictionary*, was elected to the Rawlinson and Bosworth Chair of Anglo-Saxon in a part-time capacity.

The title of Raleigh's Chair was changed to the 'Merton Professorship of English Literature' in October 1914, as Merton increased its contribution to the endowment of the Chair and made its holder a Fellow of the college. Raleigh was not altogether reluctant to leave Magdalen, partly because he was temperamentally out of sympathy with the President, Herbert Warren. Raleigh himself was turning his back on academic interests and literary criticism, to become more and more absorbed in the war and its issues. His three sons were now at the Front, but even apart from this natural preoccupation, there was nothing inconsistent about this shift of interest. He had never divorced literature from life: his definition of a pedant was a man who did so, for whom 'knowledge was a thing apart'. His late essay on George Savile made points intentionally relevant to contemporary politics, and his pamphlets on England and the war, and on the English character, combined the same mixture of personal response and insight into the world of affairs: the same desiderata he had once laid down as indispensable for understanding Shakespeare. After the war he felt deeply honoured when he was commissioned to write the official history of *The War in the Air*, and it was after returning from the Middle East with material for this work that he died of typhoid fever on 13 May 1922.

Nevertheless, one of Raleigh's final moves in the English School was as significant as anything he had done before. Towards the end of the first academic year after the war, in the spring of 1919, a step was taken to fill the vacant Merton Chair of English Language and Literature. Joseph Wright, in conference with H. T. Gerrans, the Secretary for the Local Examinations, proposed an alteration in the Statute governing the duties of the Professor. As it had stood since 1885, the Statute was quite unspecific about the nature of the Chair in relation to the other English posts created since then:

The Merton Professor of English Language and Literature shall lecture and give instruction on the history and criticism of English Language and Literature, and on the works of approved English authors.

Wright and Gerrans wished to make the Statute provide that the Professor should give instruction in the philology and history of the English language, as illustrated by English literature between the Norman Conquest and the period of Chaucer. They were both members of the Hebdomadal Council, while Raleigh was not, and their proposals were made without consulting Raleigh or Firth: when Raleigh heard of them, he wrote a letter of protest to the Council. This letter, dated 15 May 1919, sets forth Raleigh's own views on the kind of professor that was wanted, and by so doing envisages in the appointment an opportunity of bridging that gap in the school between the philological approach to early literature and the critical and historical approach to modern literature.

Raleigh pointed out that Napier's lectures had been useful only to students of the language, who were becoming even fewer among the post-war influx of students. For those primarily interested in literature, he complained, 'who are the bulk of the School, no competent teaching in the first eight centuries of

English Literature has been available, and the School, as a School of Literature, has suffered enormously from the lack of such teaching'. The appointment should therefore be made, he affirmed, with the needs of these students chiefly in mind, and he went on to outline the broader scope in which medieval English literature should be considered and taught:

That Literature has been called a faint reflection in a turbid medium of the thought and art of Medieval Latin and Medieval French. 'There was always Latin literature at the back of everything,' says Professor W. P. Ker, 'with Boethius coming clear through the Middle Ages, to be translated by Queen Elizabeth in her turn, after Chaucer and King Alfred. There was always French literature to control and give direction to the English.' Though Medieval English Literature cannot compare in importance with either of its originals, yet it has its own interest. 'It contains and preserves,' says Professor Ker again, 'in a better and completer form than elsewhere, the common ideas, the intellectual and educational ground-work of the Middle Ages.' Plainly, the man who professes it must be a good French and Latin scholar. He must be able to read English in all its stages, and, in addition, he must have something more than a hearsay acquaintance with Scholasticism and French medieval poetry. There is much for him to do. The literature of the Court of King Henry II of England, at which Court so many of the great romantic themes were shaped, has found no historian. Here is a business which belongs peculiarly to the Universities. The man who is to do it cannot be a philologist in the narrow sense.

Moreover, Raleigh was characteristically opposed to a rigid prescription of duties: flexibility and a free hand for the professoriate were still essential if the school was to develop on the right lines:

The great evil of all these elaborate prescriptions of duties is that they make it impossible to get a first-rate man. The great danger of an English School is that, lacking first-rate men, it easily becomes a mechanism, fed by second-rate talent. For the uses of a University it is very much better to get a good man and let him follow his bent in teaching, than to get a pliable inferior man and prescribe to him elaborate duties. ... The vacancy of the Merton Chair gives the University an opportunity to complete the School of English Language and Literature in such a way that it shall be the chief English School of these islands.

The letter, and in particular these closing remarks, are of interest above and beyond the occasion which produced it. It reminds us incidentally of Raleigh's unconsummated ambition to write his own book on Chaucer, to have included such a chapter as 'What the Philologists should tell us about Chaucer and don't'. It is also a hope for a better integrated school in the future than had been possible in the economic astringency of the pre-war years. But henceforth, when the colleges began to appoint their own tutors in English, how many of them would be persuaded to choose a 'pliable inferior man' to teach the whole gamut of the literature syllabus, a burden previously shared between those 'following their own bent' under the centralized system of the Fund?

However, the world has always been short of W. P. Kers. Henry Cecil Wyld, who came from Liverpool to the Merton Chair in 1920, was scarcely the kind of professor Raleigh had in mind, though he was a philologist of progressive ideas, sharing Raleigh's desire to make the Oxford School the centre of English studies in England. Wyld's Inaugural Lecture, delivered in February 1921, was devoted to a programme for research in language studies:[27] 'the first and last word in our aspirations for the future progress of our studies is Research'. He reviewed the failure of English universities to produce any body of advanced work on their own language, and outlined his plans for training scholars of English philology. There was a welcome criticism of the examination system and its effects upon teaching:

> If we thought more in terms of studies, and less in those of examina-
> tions, if it were understood that the student's prime aim was not to
> 'prepare' for the examinations, but to learn his subject so far as the time
> at his disposal would permit, the intellectual atmosphere would be
> healthier and more bracing than it sometimes is at present.

Wyld wanted to 'give some insight into the methods of research in the pre-graduate stage', and to allow students to develop their particular interests without having to spend so much of their time on aspects of the syllabus for which they had little use:

[27] *Oxford Lectures on University Studies, 1906–1921*, n.d., H. C. K. Wyld, 'English Philology in English Universities'.

I cannot help feeling that when both Literature and Philology are insisted upon for a University examination, there is a danger that the student may be harassed by being compelled constantly to turn aside from those pursuits in which lies his chief delight, and that his studies in both subjects may suffer—especially that in which he ought most to excel.

He was prepared to see the two sides of the school draw even further apart, and yet his own work on the history of the language shows that this history did not end with Chaucer, and that philology could have some bearing on our interests in later literature. Wyld's Inaugural Lecture contained a brave and ambitious programme, though Oxford had traditionally drawn too great a distinction between undergraduate studies and more advanced work to allow such a scheme to be implemented. It is a clear indication, however, of the direction in which both literary and linguistic studies in the English School were moving, until the huge post-war increase in undergraduates suddenly and completely altered the situation.

The school expanded very rapidly after the war. In addition to Dr. Simpson's Lectureship, the three Professorships, and the Goldsmith Readership, there was a second Lectureship in Literature, held by R. J. E. Tiddy until he was killed in action in 1916, and renewed in 1919 for Thomas Seccombe; and there was also a Lectureship in Language to which C. T. Onions was appointed in 1920. In addition to these university posts, and the occasional lecturers and tutors paid per course, there were nine tutors in the women's colleges at the beginning of 1920. But these were scarcely sufficient to deal with the sudden rise in the number of undergraduates, as illustrated by the following table of candidates in the Final Examinations:

1911: 13 men 22 women	1920: 6 men (21 took a special shortened Honours Course)
1912: 19 men 26 women	1921: 34 men 38 women (78 took the short course)
1913: 18 men 17 women	1922: 43 men 46 women (27 took the short course)
1914: 12 men 25 women	1923: 50 men 52 women

These figures must be trebled to arrive at the approximate number of undergraduates in the school at any given time: thus, in Michaelmas Term 1919, there were 152 men and 118 women taking the normal Honours course. A preliminary examination was introduced for first-year students in 1920. At the beginning of 1919, there were also seventeen men and two women reading for the B.Litt., four of them being Oxford graduates.

These large numbers, and the vacant fellowships created by the war, were soon to induce the colleges to provide their own teachers of English. The stability of the school no longer depended on the English Fund; moreover, such a scheme was not designed to cope with the swollen size of the post-war school. In 1926, therefore, a Statute was introduced to close the Fund, the balance remaining to be administered by the University Chest, and the interest yielded to be used for the English Library. Something was lost, however, in the process of change. Ironically, the call to make Oxford serve the needs of the nation, which had been a battle-cry of the champions of an English School in the 1880's, was now to jeopardize the principles on which that school had been built. Firth had declared in 1909 that 'the business of a School is not to train men for examination but to rear scholars'.[28] Raleigh, in the face of the post-war inflation of the school, said that 'he wanted to attract only people with a special bent for literature and did not covet the position aspired to by the History School, an alternative to "Greats" '.[29] But Oxford's traditional distrust of undergraduate specialization now found a strange ally in the attitude to 'English Literature' as an instrument of general culture, and the heyday of Raleigh's school passed with its chief architect.

It would be false to pretend that Oxford became the Mecca of English studies for which Raleigh had hoped and planned. As other Schools developed after the war, particularly in Cambridge, so the debate on the nature and function of English studies was renewed; it has remained open, much to the benefit of scholars

[28] C. H. Firth, op. cit., p. 47.
[29] Raleigh's evidence before the Board of Education Departmental Committee on the Teaching of English, given on 23 October 1919. A copy of the Manuscript Report of Evidence was given by C. H. Firth to the English Library in Oxford, and I have used this here and in Appendix II.

and their pupils. The Oxford School has had no monopoly of orthodoxy in the subsequent history of English studies, but it has above all continued to recognize that the intrinsic attractiveness of our rich and varied literature is its greatest value as a subject of study. This was Raleigh's conception of the spirit informing his school, though there were puritans in his day and since, and not in Oxford alone, who regarded this inherent attractiveness of the subject with the gravest suspicion. It has always been too easy to transpose the study of literature into the study of some ancillary topic, but Raleigh left behind him a school which demonstrated that literary study is itself a demanding and complex subject, and that academic rigour is not the peculiar prerogative of less alluring disciplines.

The Oxford English School grew to maturity under special but temporary conditions, and Raleigh and his colleagues co-operated to exploit these advantages and opportunities skilfully. Their efforts proved that the spirit of Jowett and the shade of Mark Pattison could be reconciled. When circumstances changed after the Great War, partly as a result of the very success of the school, partly because a university and its faculties do not exist for their own convenience, it became much more difficult to control the future of the school; but there were those who continued to integrate and direct its work, none with greater distinction than the late David Nichol Smith, during his long tenure of the Merton Chair of English Literature from 1929 to 1946. The old jealousies between the colleges and the university burn less fiercely than they did in the days of the fly-sheets, but if there is a lesson to be found in this history, it is that the sense of purpose and capacity for development, which are necessary for the continuing vitality of a school in all its departments, could and probably can still only come from a leadership which is a benevolent despotism. At least the distinctive character of the school was formed by a caucus that might be described and remembered as 'the Gyant Race, before the Flood'.

IX

FROM CAMBRIDGE TO BRIGHTON

THE subsequent history of English studies continued with their gradual emergence in Cambridge, where other men and conditions framed an English School with a notably different character from that of Oxford. One of the architects of the Cambridge School, the late E. M. W. Tillyard, has left us an intimate account of its development in his memoir, *The Muse Unchained* (1958); as this title suggests, the growth of Cambridge English studies was a slow process of emancipation. Originally, in 1878, the subject was yoked under the Special Board for Medieval and Modern Languages, in what Churton Collins denounced as a 'degrading vassalage to philology'. Nearly fifty years passed before English studies entered the promised land, with a Tripos which allowed the undergraduate to avoid if he wished both philology and literature before the time of Chaucer. There were four principal phases in this progress (if that word may be used without provocation), marked successively by the Special Board set up in 1878, the separation of English from other languages in the Tripos regulations of 1890, the new Tripos of 1917, and finally the innovations of 1926, when the school reached its modern form.

At Oxford the English School was born out of the divergent interests of college and university; in Cambridge the traditional division of studies for the first degree into Part I and Part II, and the absence of any central discipline in the humanities of a prestige comparable with Oxford's Greats, both played an important part in moulding the spirit and structure of English studies there. The two-part degree enabled a subject to be divided into two or more self-contained courses, and thus created the conditions by which English was first separated from other medieval and modern languages, then divided into sections which permitted a wider scope within each, modern or medieval, literary or historical.

Originally in 1882, English was one obligatory part of an Ordinary Degree in Modern Languages. Candidates were examined in four papers: Composition, History of the Language, a period of literary history, and prescribed texts studied partly from a philological point of view. After 1886, much to Churton Collins's disgust, philology still dominated English studies, when Medieval and Modern Languages rose to the dignity of a full Tripos. In 1891, however, the regulations were changed to create two Sections in English: Section B confined to medieval language and literature and related languages, and Section A which included a paper on Shakespeare and one and a half papers on literature after 1500. In 1900 the literary content of Section A was increased to two papers on English literature as far as 1832. Proposals in 1909 to bifurcate Section A, and so to introduce more literature into the available choices, were rejected by the Senate, but they illustrate how the combinations possible under the bi-partite degree system facilitated the separate organization of literary studies. In 1917 Section A was re-arranged with options, so that in future the English part of the Tripos could be taken without any linguistic study and without any knowledge of literature before 1350. This was the reform which introduced the papers on 'Life, Literature, and Thought', soon to get a mixed reception when representatives of the Cambridge School gave evidence in 1920 to the Board of Education's Committee on the Teaching of English.[1] 'Life, Literature, and Thought' indicated the distinctive bent of English studies in Cambridge. As yet, however, candidates for Section A had to combine English with another subject to complete their degree, and it was not until 1926 that a degree in English alone became possible. In that year the English Faculty Board was created, and a Section C introduced papers on tragedy, literary criticism, special subjects, and a new branch of study, practical criticism. By combining Section A with Section C a new and independent course in English was created. 'Bliss was it in that dawn to be alive.'

Of the personalities involved in these developments, Tillyard's memoir gives a leading part to H. M. Chadwick, the

[1] See Appendix II, pp. 181–2.

Professor of Anglo-Saxon, whose wide interests in archaeology and cultural history led him to distrust the value of philology in undergraduate studies, and so to press for the divorce of literature from language in the reformed courses. Chadwick became Professor in 1912, after the death of W. W. Skeat, who had held the Chair since it was established in 1878. English studies might have developed very differently if, in that same year of 1912, Chadwick's colleague, the new Professor of English Literature, had been Herbert Grierson instead of Arthur Quiller-Couch. Grierson's distinction as the editor of Donne, according to Tillyard, would have earned him the Chair if the election had been decided purely on academic grounds. 'Q' was neither a scholar nor an administrator: Grierson might not have shared so readily in the enthusiasms which led to the new syllabus of 1917.

When the proposals of 1917 were made known to Raleigh in Oxford, he disapproved of them, as Tillyard says 'for reasons unknown to me', though he welcomed the move to dissociate English studies from modern languages. The reasons for Raleigh's mixed response are not difficult to guess: he regarded the study of English language and literature as a branch of learning in its own right, but was suspicious of attempts to make it supplant classical studies as the central discipline of the humanities. For this was what was in the minds of the Cambridge reformers. The changes were made in the hope that Classics would become the recognized preparation for the modern side of the English course, just as in Oxford Classical Moderations preceded admission to the English School. But the Oxford School was in no sense a substitute for Greats: the difference between English in Oxford and English in Cambridge is epitomized in the contrasting emphases of 'Language and Literature' and 'Life, Literature, and Thought'. With the further changes of 1926, including the appearance of the 'English Moralists' paper and of practical criticism, English at Cambridge assumed its distinctive form. By recruiting teachers such as G. C. Coulton, Basil Willey, and I. A. Richards, with their respective interests in social history, the history of ideas, and psychology, the Cambridge School was designed to provide a more philosophical approach to literature.

The time also helped to give the Cambridge School its distinctive bias. English studies at Oxford were developed during the ten years between the appointment of Raleigh and the beginning of the Great War; the moving spirit behind the reforms of the Cambridge Tripos in 1917 was an anticipation of the post-war situation, when the numbers wishing to read English rose so suddenly. Here, it seemed to the architects of Cambridge English studies, were both the pressure and the opportunity to make the study of English literature the central discipline of modern humane education.

Modern it certainly was in Cambridge. 'Practical criticism' was a reflection of the new attitude of mental toughness which generally characterized post-war intellectual life. Tillyard suggested that it was in part a reaction to the vague impressionist rhapsodies that often passed for criticism before the war; he indicated its kinship with the critical essays of T. S. Eliot, then first appearing, to the great excitement of the younger generation of poetry readers. Tillyard also pointed out the extent to which practical criticism was derived from Freudian psychology, and from the linguistic philosophy of G. E. Moore in Cambridge.[2] It was no accident that I. A. Richards, the chief promoter of the new critical technique, had read the Moral Sciences Tripos under Moore. Probably practical criticism has been the most influential and distinctive contribution which the Cambridge School has made to English studies, but like any new technique it has been open to abuse, particularly where it has been used as an instrument in the examination system. Tillyard himself complained that in the hands of clever but immature students it has often dwindled to a kind of game, in which the 'rules' could soon be learned and applied in a mechanical fashion. Exaggerated claims have been made for its use as a touchstone of innate literary sensibility, but in fact the flexibility and subtlety of perceptive critical analysis require not only a natural aptitude but in addition a wide experience of different kinds of literature. Since the 1920's we have been made more aware of the dangers attending practical criticism, in particular of its tendency to overrate the virtues of complexity

[2] Op. cit., pp. 81–100.

and ambiguity. The writers who yield most readily to an analysis of their imagery and concealed meanings get the highest marks, while literature of a plainer texture or more obvious structure is made to seem comparatively less attractive. Practical criticism came into vogue with the revived interest in seventeenth-century metaphysical poetry and with the discovery of Gerard Manley Hopkins, and its preoccupation with metaphor and imagery indicated also its association with imagist poetry. In recent years, however, the range of critical analysis has been extended, and a recovered interest in poetic syntax is one sign that the school of imagists has perhaps had its day.

Nevertheless, analytic techniques have permanently affected the course of academic criticism, and, as the work of Dr. Leavis exemplifies, they have been assimilated into the more traditional form of the critical essay. Doubts have been cast on the value of practical criticism as an exercise by itself, or as a substitute for extensive reading, but, adapted to the writing of criticism, its methods of close analysis have greatly extended the power of the critic to demonstrate in local effects the characteristics of longer works. 'Comparison and analysis', as T. S. Eliot put it, 'are the chief tools of the critic'; though he also indicated the limitations of practical criticism when he added, 'You must know what to compare and what to analyse'.[3]

Practical criticism was in one sense a new kind of rhetorical study: the work of I. A. Richards, however pseudo-scientific it may seem in retrospect, has provided much of the terminology used in modern criticism. The recent revival of academic interest in Renaissance rhetoric has been due at least in part to the challenge of this unhistorical, and as some would claim misleading, method of analysis.

If practical criticism represented the element of intensive discipline in Cambridge English studies, analogous to the traditional rôle of 'language' in Oxford, it was balanced by the extensive study of 'Life, Literature, and Thought'. The social and intellectual background here assumes an importance equal to that of literature itself: one is reminded of A. J. Scott's declaration in

[3] T. S. Eliot, *Selected Essays* (1932), 3rd edn. 1951, 'The Function of Criticism', p. 33.

1848 that 'a poet of the first order is the voice of a great era'.[4] Since Scott's day, few have denied that literature is better understood in relation to its cultural and historical setting: in Oxford, too, English was being studied in its historical context. But in the Oxford School literature and language were the only subjects of examination, and if the examination syllabus is a good indication of distinctive emphasis, then the papers on 'Life, Literature, and Thought', together with that on the English Moralists, showed that in Cambridge literature was to be chiefly studied as the transmission of those moral and cultural ideals through which the past nourishes the present.

Nevertheless, it is always easy to overstate the differences between Oxford and Cambridge, and in each university English studies as they are actually taught are obviously broad enough to permit considerable variety and flexibility. Yet in comparison with Oxford, the new Cambridge School may well have seemed designed to study a subject much wider and more diffuse than English literature, to embrace in effect the whole span of modern English thought and culture; while on the other hand, to the architects of the Cambridge School, conscious of its long struggle for emancipation, there appeared, as Dr. Tillyard implies, something very specialized and old-fashioned about English studies in Oxford. Cambridge rejected Old English as too remote to be of any direct relevance to a modern discipline in the humanities, while the position of Old English in the Oxford course was due not so much to a planned and coherent scheme of studies, as to historical accident and vested interest. Although it was true that arguments for the retention of Old English and of language studies were *post facto* justifications, it would be unjust to dismiss these elements as 'philology'. The examination syllabus of the Oxford School showed that Old English was to be studied for its literary value, and that the history of the language was a separate study, related to literature from Chaucer to modern times. These gave the Oxford School its distinctive bias of historical study, and illustrated its belief that matters of specific literary interest were the main subject of study, and provided of themselves a

4 See Chapter II, p. 26.

sufficient basis for examination. A historical interest in language did not mean a concern with what Walter Raleigh scornfully described as 'hypothetical sound-shiftings in the primeval German forests',[5] but rather it implied an awareness of changes in meaning, of uses of syntax, and above all of those changing attitudes to the language in its relations with literature which counted for so much in English writing at least between Spenser and Wordsworth. Old English, it was argued in Oxford, was included on its own literary merits: *Beowulf* was worth studying first and foremost as a work of art written in England. In practice, however, the teaching of language and of Old English in Oxford has not always realized these ideals. The historical study of the language has too often been allowed to dwindle to text-grubbing and no more, while in teaching Old English a greater effort should have been made from the start to relate the achievements of the philologists, textual scholars, historians, and archaeologists to the literary values to which most students are capable of responding. But to compare the range and variety of English studies as they are actually taught in Oxford and Cambridge would be greatly to reduce differences between the two schools. Could it be maintained with conviction that the Oxford School has produced more 'specialists', while those who have taken the English Tripos in Cambridge possess a broader moral and cultural awareness? We scarcely expect a philosophy graduate to be wiser than a student of law or of sociology by virtue of his training: too much depends on the mental equipment which is brought to the subject. The academic status of Greats in nineteenth-century Oxford was inseparable from the social status of the public schools, and this was surely a much more significant factor in producing the redoubtable 'Greats man' than any inherent superiority of ancient history and philosophy over modern history or English studies as academic disciplines. Yet evidently it is often assumed that a broad extensive curriculum will produce an unspecialized, comprehensive mind, and correspondingly that a narrow intensive study will result in a limited, specialist mentality. There is no such simple correlation. If English studies in

---

[5] *The Teaching of English in England*, 1921, p. 218.

Cambridge were to take the place of Classics as an education in the humanities, then first they had to attract the kind of student who in the past would have read Classics, and this involved rather more than merely drawing up a syllabus of a certain kind.

While the new school recruited teachers and scholars of such heterogeneous interests and temperaments, it lacked a highly centralized system of administration, such as the English Fund in Oxford before the war. Elements of faction and internal dissension were inevitable, and in his account Tillyard described some of the disagreements which affected the early leadership of the school. These quarrels are of interest only as they illustrate the various sectors of influence in Cambridge English studies, but perhaps none was more significant than the now legendary mutual antipathy between King's College and Downing. The grounds of those differences are well known, even outside Cambridge, and they illuminate one distinctive aspect of the Cambridge School: its close ties with the literary movements of the day. King's had personal associations with the Bloomsbury Circle, and, if he had survived the Great War, Rupert Brooke would have been a leading figure in the new school. Dr. F. R. Leavis, on the other hand, was an admirer of I. A. Richards and one of the first critics to recognize the literary revolution promoted by T. S. Eliot. And Dr. Leavis himself has become a part of the history of twentieth-century literature: he has had much more influence upon modern critical doctrine than he has enjoyed at home in the Cambridge English School.

This, then, is not the place to discuss Dr. Leavis as a critic. Yet nobody has argued more cogently about the place of English studies in the university, and his views call for consideration however summary it must be. In 1943, as the Second World War was approaching its final stages, Dr. Leavis published *Education and the University*, a powerful statement of the need to make the ancient universities fulfil their rôle as representatives of a humane tradition in modern society. In the chapter called 'A Sketch for an English School', he outlined a programme for English studies which would constitute an education for a cultural élite, such as that formerly available in Classics. Though the differences of emphasis are important, the chief principles of the plan are not far removed from some of the distinctive ideals of the Cambridge School, and, indeed, Dr. Leavis was at pains to show that his proposals did not involve radical reforms in the existing structure of the school so much as a more thorough realization of its possibilities. The relationship which he proposed between a Part I intended to give students a wide basis of literary experience with the necessary grounding in critical techniques, and a Part II devoted to more advanced studies in a particular period ('Life, Literature, and Thought'), is reminiscent of the relationship between Honour Moderations and Greats in Oxford. Dr. Leavis's conception of a cultural élite is also akin to Coleridge's 'National Church', which was 'to preserve the stores and to guard the treasures of past civilization', an influential idea in the development of English studies, though Dr. Leavis is more concerned with the wise man than with the learned. His contention that the Classics have had their day, however, is less convincingly illustrated by his sardonic remarks about the poor literary tastes shared by 'persons of undisturbed classical training'.[6] A liking for A. E. Housman, C. E. Montague, or P. G. Wodehouse is perhaps hard to forgive, but it really represents the taste of a social class, and in any case is no firm indication of an incapacity to cope with 'the important choices of actual life'.

A more convincing part of *Education and the University* is its vigorous indictment of the examination system, which, as Dr. Leavis shows, not only puts a premium on the most superficial and irrelevant skills, but also impedes the proper business of learning (particularly where time is limited) by inducing pupil and teacher to conspire against the examination.[7] In Dr. Leavis's view, the proper business of an English School, the essential discipline, should be literary criticism, and its object the trained sensibility:

To talk of training and sensibility and intelligence may seem to have narrowly limiting suggestion, as if it were merely a matter of 'practical criticism' work upon short poems and odds and ends. But of course that kind of work can have continuous developments into the com-

---

[6] Op. cit., p. 39.   [7] Ibid., p. 44.

pletest kind of interpretative and evaluation criticism. . . . The kind of work advocated entails, in its irreplaceable discipline, a most independent and responsible exercise of intelligence and judgment on the part of the student. The more advanced the work the more unmistakably is the judgment that is concerned inseparable from that profoundest sense of relative value which determines, or should determine, the important choices of actual life.[8]

This is a vital part of the book, and represents Dr. Leavis's particular and uncompromising stress upon the traditional belief that we are somehow wiser and better for our reading of great literature, just as the confessed aim of all education has always been in one way or another to equip us for 'the important choices of actual life'. Nevertheless the stress is a narrow one: it is difficult to see how the discipline of literary criticism is superior in this respect to the disciplines of moral philosophy or historical scholarship, for example, and unless it is indeed superior there seems little reason why English studies should be peculiarly fitted to become the chief underprop of humane education, as Dr. Leavis would have them to be. Since his proposals have never been implemented, we have still to discover whether the literary critics trained under these conditions would be markedly better epuipped than other educated men, but the notion seems rather improbable. As a race, the great critics of the past have not been particularly distinguished from their fellow men for their adroitness in dealing with 'the important choices of actual life'.

Another question that remains is whether Dr. Leavis's scheme would be desirable, supposing it to be successful. The trained discrimination and the responsible sense of values, which would distinguish Dr. Leavis's cultural élite, are qualities to be prized: but so are the humility, tolerance, flexibility, and intellectual curiosity which we may expect a literary education to foster. As the guardians of our cultural values, Dr. Leavis's élite would be an impressive body, but without these other qualities they might be a trifle inclined to spiritual arrogance and self-righteousness. In fact a School of English usually provides more than what Dr. Leavis emphasizes as an education in reading, and for the under-

[8] Op. cit., p. 34.

graduate regular essay work is an important part of the business of learning to assimilate the literary experience.

In the twenty years since *Education and the University* appeared, the expansion of university education has passed through one phase, and entered a second. In the first of these, following the end of the Second World War, university colleges which formerly prepared students for the London external degrees achieved the status of full universities. During the current phase, several wholly new universities have been created, beginning with North Staffordshire in 1949. Of all the changes and experiments which new universities are free to make, none is proving of greater interest than the introduction of Arts courses that cut across the boundaries of the traditional disciplines, and attempt to embrace wider areas of study within a single degree structure. This shape of things to come is a challenge to more conservative assumptions about the very nature of university studies.

It is difficult to place in true perspective the present multiplicity of ideas and arguments about the proper studies of mankind, but the feeling grows that we have reached a crisis of confidence in the conventional single-subject honours degree. While the time is not ripe to judge the success of the new broader-based courses, they are an implicit recognition of the fact that many of the students who now arrive at the university are ill-prepared for a traditional single-subject discipline.

The increased demand for higher education comes not only from a larger population in the relevant age-group, but also from a higher proportion of that age-group. Under this pressure, where the number of teachers is limited, the conventional pattern of sixth-form education has collapsed; to the problem of greater numbers has been added at an ever-increasing pace the stress of examination-work, since the intensified competition for university places has taken the form of achieving progressively higher grades in two or three subjects at the Advanced Level of the G.C.E. In most universities the disparity between the minimum requirements for matriculation and the examination grades demanded for admission grows wider each year. It is a familiar and distressing picture; the consequence in educational terms has been the almost total disappearance of that phase of developing intellectual curiosity and broadening interests necessary as a preparation for university study. The comparative freedom and responsibility formerly allowed to a small sixth form, with opportunities for self-directed study and individual supervision, are often virtually impossible when a large class has to be driven through the narrow hoop of prescribed texts for the examination. Conditions conspire to produce a freshman who is tired and jaded after the supreme efforts of securing a university place, who has little or no learning outside his examination syllabus, and who has neither the maturity nor the self-reliance that could once be expected after a sixth-form education. The root causes of the situation in which many students have too narrow a basis for tackling the traditional type of honours degree are thus both the thin spread of sixth-form teaching and the present use of the G.C.E. examination as a selector for university entrance. It is difficult to believe that this appalling state of affairs was either inevitable or that it can be allowed to remain permanently, but the best advice we have suggests that it will not be rectified before 1980.

An important distinction should be made between this appraisal of the effects of expansion, as they concern the rôle of the single-subject degree, and the mere prejudice that since university education in England has always been the privilege of the few, only the few are capable of attaining to it, and that greater numbers will of themselves lead to lower standards. Certainly there is no reason to suppose that the inter-disciplinary studies of the new universities imply inferior academic standards, though this cry is heard whenever new subjects and methods are introduced into the pattern of higher education. As always, more depends upon the attractions which the various branches of study, and the various universities, hold for the ablest minds. Yet, while some universities have begun to question the place of the single-subject honours degree, it still bears a gilt-edged prestige in English life, and because the degree in several subjects has been in the past a general or pass degree, it is associated with a lower level of attainment. The general degree, however, has often comprised a bundle of unrelated and fragmentary studies, while the 'area studies' of the new universities are planned to integrate into schools those historical, linguistic, philosophical, and literary studies which are structurally distinct in the older institutions. Indeed, it is difficult to see how these broad-based courses can be introduced into the traditional kind of Arts Faculty unless the whole pattern of government and the organization of teaching are also changed; the abstraction of elements from a number of disciplines in a paper syllabus is quite inadequate by itself to secure a properly integrated course of study.

So far I have argued that the crisis of confidence in the specialist honours degree is closely related to some of the more unfortunate effects of university expansion. But, of course, the new developments in 'area studies' are not merely the products of a reaction against 'specialist training' in favour of 'general education'. This alone could not account for the evident vitality and enthusiasm which invest the new universities. Teaching always reflects shifts of interest in scholarship and the emergence of new branches of learning: an axiom obvious in the natural sciences is perhaps less clearly defined but also true in the humanities. The swing away from 'language and literature' towards 'area studies' reflects the growth of such modern fields of study as comparative linguistics, comparative literature (including the literature of the United States), and the history of ideas, in each of which American scholarship has taken the initiative.

These new branches and combinations of study restore to the specialist disciplines a balance which was formerly provided by classical studies. Originally the Schools of English in Oxford and Cambridge were each designed in the belief that those choosing the subject would have devoted the first phase of their university studies to Classics. The Oxford School was not intended to supplant Greats, though English studies in Cambridge began to move in that direction when literature took a place alongside 'life and thought' —a prototype of 'area studies'. In *Education and the University* Dr. Leavis suggested the introduction of a dissertation on a special period (he cited the seventeenth century), in which the student would have an opportunity to explore more thoroughly the relations between literature and society. Of course, students of

English literature have always been expected to show an awareness of a wider historical and intellectual context in so far as this helps to illuminate the character of the literature they are reading, but at the undergraduate level this information is usually provided in the pre-digested form of modern surveys, and figures only as 'background' to the literary texts. There are two significant points of difference between the Oxford-type course in 'language and literature' and the character of English studies in the new interdisciplinary schools: whereas the former is based on a continuous historical sequence from earliest times to within one or two generations of the present, in 'area studies' a number of selected periods are presented 'in section', and also rather more emphasis is placed on the modern period. The main object of study in 'language and literature' is self-evident; I have already discussed how and why theory and practice are divergent here, as 'language' has tended to merge with the study of medieval literature. But where English studies form a single-subject degree course, the chief interest is assumed to be in the literary text as a work of art, and not as documentary evidence for social history or as part of the history of ideas.

Weighing the gain and loss to English studies in these broad-based courses, it seems much to everybody's advantage that some English language and literature can now be studied in a context that does not demand the special aptitudes and enthusiasms for which the traditional honours course is more particularly fitted. Many of those who pass through our university schools of English have a high but general and undifferentiated academic ability, and discover quite early in their undergraduate careers that they derive no particular pleasure or profit from such an abundant literary diet as forms the staple of the specialist honours course. More of a choice *à la carte* would often be better digested. The study of English assumes a love of literature even before a love of learning, and this above all is why it is not suited to the rôle in which it has sometimes been cast, as the successor to the old classical education. The new Arts courses, on the other hand, where literature is combined with history and philosophy, are more truly the modern counterpart of Greats.

If, as seems probable, the single-subject degree will lose its near-monopoly of university studies, then the numbers taking the traditional kind of English honours course will proportionately decline, and this will be a change for the better. There is still a place for the school of language and literature, and indeed there seems no likelihood of its total disappearance. But it will attract only those more deliberately motivated towards a literary discipline. What is needed is greater diversity in the pattern of university studies, and an increased number of options within the structure of the honours degree, in place of the fixed single-subject course. It should be possible to achieve this increased flexibility without sacrificing a proper standard of integration between the available options of the syllabus. 'Area studies' will quite possibly preserve a better balance than that usually found between 'language' and 'literature'. A large university is in a better position to diversify its teaching in such a way that the substance of the traditional honours course may exist alongside the inter-disciplinary studies. But even so the boards of studies would have to be organized to secure a genuine 'parity of esteem' between the multiple options offered for the first degree.

The last great phase of university expansion, during the nineteenth century, has bequeathed us an examination system still unchanged in its essentials, and examinations have a way of thwarting the best-laid schemes of study. When the Oxford English School was in the making sixty years ago, its immediate object was to transform the study of English literature from an illiberal kind of examination fodder to a proper branch of learning. But as the subject expands and moves ahead, the ineluctable examiners are always in close pursuit, devising ways to trap and imprison the free spirit of inquiry within a cloven pine. 'There are two Days of Judgment,' wrote Walter Raleigh, 'and Final Schools are the less important.' If examinations must remain, and it is difficult to see how we can do without them, the kind of ability they measure may at least be extended at university level by reducing the emphasis on the three-hour paper answered from memory. Dr. Leavis's suggestion, of introducing a dissertation on a special subject as part of the requirements for a degree, has two features which recommend it. By requiring a more sustained piece of work, involving a more entensive use of first-hand material and a more thorough investigation of the subject than the usual undergraduate essay produces, not only does the dissertation exercise a different range of abilities, but these abilities are better related to more mature and advanced study. Distinction in the conventional examination for the first degree does not always indicate the good research scholar: the undergraduate dissertation could serve as a more reliable means of preparing and selecting for post-graduate work.

The graduate who remains at the university for a further two or three years is usually seeking to equip himself for an academic career. His training at this stage needs to be more professional, for as he extends and deepens his knowledge he also has to acquire those methods and standards of scholarship which will enable him to make throughout his career a sustained contribution to the advancement of his branch of learning. The normal qualification for an academic post is a higher degree, and traditionally in English studies this involves either a written thesis on a narrow topic of research or an editorial presentation of a text. Everyone knows how often the subjects of graduate research are trivial or arid: this system fosters a most illiberal and mechanical view of scholarship. Indeed it is not really a system at all, but a haphazard and inefficient process, in which the wind bloweth as it listeth. Two or three years of advanced study may provide no real training outside a very narrow field of inquiry, and many are those who fall by the wayside. Yet the future promotion of English studies depends upon the quality of the next generation of scholars.

Many schools of English are too small to possess adequate resources for graduate training on a proper scale, but, of the greater universities, Oxford has a particular importance as a centre of advanced studies. From its origins the Oxford English School was concerned to foster research, and graduate courses were organized accordingly. The B.Litt. programme has attracted students from America as well as from other British universities because it has provided a planned introduction to the special skills and principles of scholarship. The view has generally been taken in Oxford that a thesis of itself is an inadequate preparation, and often inevitably immature: 'a piece of 'prentice work', as Nichol Smith called it. Consequently, by taking seriously its responsibilities towards graduate studies, and regarding them as certainly of no less importance than the undergraduate school, English studies in Oxford have enjoyed a status less parochial than that of their counterparts elsewhere. Now that so much of the important work in English studies comes from the United States, more than ever we need graduate schools of the Oxford and American types, planned to give a training in research which can lead to a truly professional awareness of how this form of study may best be promoted.

By virtue of their resources and traditions, Oxford, Cambridge, and London bear a special responsibility as centres of research. But other universities are not likely to accept the impoverishment of their proper functions which would result if all their best graduates left them to complete a course of advanced study elsewhere. The expansion of higher education, and the problem of continuing to staff our universities adequately, aggravate the need for reappraising the whole question of graduate studies on a national scale. A few universities have already followed the example of the Oxford B.Litt. in providing a broader introduction to methods of research alongside the conventional supervision of a thesis. It should be possible, however, to devise a system of closer co-operation between our universities for the training of graduates, and to mobilize the diversity of their resources. In this way, for instance, more research students could be temporarily seconded from the smaller universities to attend the special classes in advanced study available only in the greater centres, while the burden of the thesis work could remain home-based. Although few libraries are adequate to meet the requirements of a student whose special interests lie in the medieval or renaissance periods, there are many with an increasingly better coverage of nineteenth- and twentieth-century materials, and several with special collections of different kinds. Nevertheless, the needs of more mature research will continue to bring scholars to the few great libraries such as the Bodleian and the British Museum. At the moment they come from other universities only as time and money will allow them; indeed, it is usually easier for a foreign academic to spend a period of time in these centres of research than it is for the teacher from a provincial university. It might well be an arrangement of mutual benefit if more of the senior scholars in other universities were invited to spend a year in Oxford, Cambridge, or London, to assist in the school of graduate studies while they also furthered their own work in the libraries there. This is one of many ways in which we might profitably adapt the American example to our own conditions, for as the English system of university studies is committed to a future of change through growth, the model of the United States will serve in much the same way as did that of Germany during the last century, and subject to similar qualifications.

These prospects for change sharpen our awareness of what from the past must be kept or discarded. During the hundred years or so since English studies were first introduced into the universities, a certain pattern has emerged in the attempts to define their function and purpose. Because the literature of the past is sufficiently valuable to the present, we have thought it worthwhile to set about recovering as much of its meaning as we can, and training people how to read it, believing also that this training can fulfil the traditional aims of humane education. These articles of faith have not passed unchallenged, both by those who object to putting the Muse in chains, who feel that the austere spirit of the lecture-room may deprive literature of that imaginative delight through which it teaches, and also by those who feel that the delights of literature may deprive the lecture-room of its customary austerity. These are the Cavaliers and Roundheads in the Civil Wars of our subject, but to insist upon a necessary antipathy between the pleasures of poetry and the labours of study is to betray a very narrow view of each. There is nevertheless a delicate balance between the defined purpose and the achievement of English studies, illustrated throughout their development by the arguments about their relationship to the old classical education. From its early status as the poor man's Classics, the study of

English literature was proclaimed by nineteenth-century evangel-
ists of 'culture' and their successors as an instrument of great moral
and spiritual influence, and in their anxiety over the debased
values of an industrial democracy they invested English studies
with a special rôle at the centre of the humanities, supplanting the
declining Classics. This rôle was conceived to be the training
of a cultural élite. But, apart from the misinterpretation of the
interplay between social class, social prestige, and education, this
way of defining the purpose of English studies by their results
was misleading, because it failed to indicate at what level the
purpose operated: whether it was the purpose of the student, of
his teacher, of the compiler of the syllabus, or of Providence itself.
To approach the study of literature with the aim of becoming a
member of an élite, or a teacher, or a poet, or with any other aim
that reduces the literature to a means and not an end, is to
undermine the very conditions which make literature worth
studying. C. S. Lewis has put this point in its most succinct form:
'Those who read poetry to improve their minds will never
improve their minds by reading poetry.'[9] Purpose and result are
related only indirectly: you can take your horse to Helicon, but
you cannot make him drink. Similarly, it has never been even a
part of the purpose of English studies in this country to breed
poets and novelists, yet a significant number of the most eminent
of our living writers did read English at the university; although
it was not designed to this end, their training permitted an influence upon their creative interests. The value of a literary
education does not depend on accident, but it cannot be harnessed
to a formula.

The academic orientation of literary scholarship and criticism
has had its disadvantages, chiefly because it seems to appropriate
the great writers of the past within a small professional circle,
where the level of discussion makes little contact with the interests of that now rather melancholy figure, the 'general reader'.
Few outside the universities can follow the highly-specialized
and technical methods of academic criticism, and small wonder

[9] 'Lilies That Fester', *Twentieth Century*, April 1955. See also the rejoinder by W. W.
Robson, 'They That Have Power', in the number for June 1955.

when even the academics for whose benefit it is supposedly written find so much of this critical writing pedestrian or trivial, too often published only for the sake of publication. We shall soon have two distinct levels of literary experience existing side by side; where there is perhaps already an academic Shakespeare and a popular Shakespeare, there will also be two Dr. Johnsons and even two Dickens—a fate that neither would have contemplated with equanimity. It is not a living literature that is read only within a university library, and as the complex resources of academic scholarship are recovering the words and meanings of English writers from ancient oblivion and modern ignorance, their fruits must be made not merely available in the formal sense, but accessible to the non-specialist as well.

For such reasons the emphasis which has been placed on the peculiar and distinctive character of a training in English studies is rather a dangerous one. The evidence does not suggest that graduates of our English Schools are either more or less 'cultured' as a group than those who were trained in history, modern languages, or philosophy. In fact the study of English shares many of the educational values of other humane disciplines; in common with these, it instils a care for truth, and develops the powers of judgment and expression. The training of these qualities may be said to be its aim, in the sense that they are measured by examination in the end. Few other subjects, moreover, are able to confront the student with the raw material of his study so directly as this, and the great and immeasurable gift of English studies has been to many thousands what C. S. Lewis, this time in a different mood, described as 'the enormous extension of our being which we owe to authors'. University Schools of English have no monopoly of this experience, but their existence has allowed it to be shared more abundantly.

APPENDIX I

THE EARLY STUDY OF ENGLISH
LITERATURE IN SCOTTISH UNIVERSITIES

IT is sometimes said, especially by Scotsmen, that the academic study
of English literature began in Scotland. But questions of precedence are
not easily settled, least of all where national pride has exaggerated their
importance. For the record, however, there were Professors of English
in London and Manchester for some time before such a title first
appeared north of the border, when the Regius Chair of English Language and Literature was established at Glasgow University in 1862.
Edinburgh shortly followed suit when David Masson was appointed
Professor of Rhetoric and English Literature in 1865, before which time
the Chair had been known as that of Rhetoric and Belles Lettres:
moreover, Masson was imported there from University College,
London. And another thirty years passed before Aberdeen (1893) and
St. Andrews (1897) possessed their Chairs of English, long after there
was any novelty in the subject.

But the Scottish claim rests on a different foundation. The distinctive
character of the four Scottish universities, with their traditional pattern
of a four-years Arts course covering an extensive field of subjects, and,
after the end of the seventeenth century, with their affiliation to secular
authorities rather than to the Church, make their historical situation
very different from that of the English universities, ancient or modern.
The Act of Union in 1707 preserved Scottish autonomy in education as
in religion, and it was during the eighteenth century that English
literature began to be studied in university classes of rhetoric and logic,
under a system which closely resembled that of the contemporary
Dissenting Academies in England. A recent historian of Scottish
university education has told us that

The crucial fact is that, by about 1700, the continuing Scottish efforts to re-
organise law and education on rational lines had achieved a considerable
measure of success, whereas the corresponding movement in England for a
utilitarian reform of law and education had failed lamentably and was being
forgotten.[1]

[1] G. E. Davie, *The Democratic Intellect*, 1961, Introductory Essay, p. xv.

Appendix I

While this is possibly a fair judgement of Oxford and Cambridge during that period, it overlooks the flourishing and progressive utilitarianism of the Dissenting Academies, which, as I have tried to show in an earlier chapter, inherited the reforming zeal and rational experimentalism of the Puritan educational thinkers. As I indicated when describing these academies,[2] there was some contact between them and the Scottish universities, but they were by no means dependent on the Scottish example for their ideals of a practical general education, which included the principles of modern science and the use of the vernacular, in contrast to the traditional study of ancient texts and the composition of Latin and Greek verses, which formed the Arts courses of the ancient English universities.

One prominent feature of the Scottish system was the importance given to philosophy, so that the various subjects were studied in their philosophical principles, before attention was paid to detailed or advanced knowledge. This was at least partly related to the fact that Scottish youths came to the universities much earlier in their development, fifteen or sixteen being the normal age. Instruction in classes and the writing and discussion of essays were methods reinforcing this emphasis upon the ability to refer back to first principles, and upon the avoidance of narrow specialisms in the Arts course. Thus the principles of rhetoric or of criticism had prior importance to the study of any literature or texts, and the practice and study of rhetoric or logic could be conducted under these conditions with greater facility in English: this was particularly so when the syllabus was extended as the Regent system gave way to the provision of separate teachers for each subject. So, at any rate, they must have thought at Marischal College in Aberdeen, for the course there in 1753 included the 'principles of criticism and *Belles Lettres*' for students in their third year, alongside spherical trigonometry, hydrostatics, optics, electricity, and other branches of science.[3]

Though it had been mooted since Andrew Melville persuaded James VI to refound Glasgow in 1577, the final abolition of 'Regenting' during the first half of the eighteenth century meant that more professorships were created in a greater variety of subjects. Edinburgh, which had been the first university to take this step in 1708, also led the way in creating a Chair of Rhetoric and Belles Lettres in 1762. Previously these subjects came within the province of the Professor of Logic, as

[2] Chapter I, p. 9., *supra*.
[3] A. Morgan, *Scottish University Studies*, 1933, p. 73.

they continued to be in the other universities; indeed, Stevenson, the Professor of Logic in Edinburgh since 1730, complained that the new Chair would deprive him of one of his most successful classes. According to the account given by H. W. Meikle,[4] this Chair had its origins outside the university itself, when in 1748 Adam Smith had delivered a course of lectures on literary subjects at the instigation of Lord Kames, and possibly, as Meikle suggests, sponsored by the Philosophical Society. At any rate, the lectures proved so popular that they were renewed in subsequent years, and came to an end only when Smith went to Glasgow in 1751 as the Professor of Logic. The lectures were revived, however, once more with the support of Lord Kames, and the mantle of Smith fell upon Robert Watson, who, we are told, had 'acquired a knowledge of the principles of philosophical or universal grammar, and prepared lectures on style and language and rhetoric'. Probably Watson had attended Adam Smith's courses, and he may even have used Smith's lecture notes, as Hugh Blair certainly did when he resumed the lectures in 1759, three years after Watson had been appointed to the Chair of Logic, Rhetoric, and Metaphysics in St. Andrews. But Blair delivered his lectures in the university, and in 1760 the Town Council, as the governing body of the university, elected him Professor of Rhetoric, a post to which the Crown gave its blessing and endowment in 1762.

Hugh Blair was one of the best known literary figures of his day, through his *Sermons*, and his championship of the *Poems of Ossian*: in which, incidentally, he rejoiced to find 'all the essential requisites of a true and regular epic', although today we prefer to associate the vogue enjoyed by this literary forgery with the growth of Romantic taste. Except that he delivered his instruction in lectures rather than classes, there is no reason to suppose that the content of Blair's teaching differed very much from the rhetorical studies of other Scottish universities at that time. His influence lasted long after he retired from the active duties of his Chair in 1784. During the previous year he had published his *Lectures on Rhetoric and Belles Lettres*, which were to go through successive editions until the middle of the next century, including that prepared for the press by Thomas Dale in 1845. Blair's reputation only faded, in fact, when the doctrines of Romanticism finally permeated the popular critical taste.

Unfortunately the success with which the Edinburgh Chair was

[4] H. W. Meikle, 'The Chair of Rhetoric and Belles Lettres', *University of Edinburgh Journal*, Autumn 1945, pp. 89–103.

inaugurated was not maintained, and English studies languished there for over fifty years after Blair's retirement. He continued to hold his Professorship in idleness until his death in 1800, when the post was offered to Sir Walter Scott, who refused it, to the everlasting loss of English studies. Instead, a piece of royal jobbery secured the Chair for Andrew Brown, who did not lecture but drew the emoluments while compiling a history of North America which he never published. So far had English studies declined into torpor, that in 1831 the first commission on Scottish universities recommended that the teaching of rhetoric should again be united with that of logic. This retrograde step was not taken, however, for after Brown's death in 1834 the Chair was given, for no discernible reason, to an advocate, George Moir, whose legal business would seemingly not permit him to do any more than his predecessor to advance the cause of English studies, and in 1840 Moir resigned.

Before concluding this phase of English studies in Scotland, mention should be made of William Richardson's *Philosophical Analysis and Illustration of Some of Shakespeare's Remarkable Characters*, published in 1774. Richardson was the Professor of Humanity (that is, Latin) in the University of Glasgow, and though his approach to Shakespeare was not that of the rhetoricians, there is something characteristic of the Scottish academic spirit in his method, 'to make poetry subservient to philosophy, and to employ it in tracing the principles of human conduct'. In Richardson, psychology and literary criticism made their bed together, a liaison that proved fertile for the interpretation of Shakespeare, but this did not disturb the marriage of rhetoric and English studies in Scotland; it is interesting to reflect, however, that this psychological approach to Shakespeare culminated 120 years later in the work of another Glasgow professor, A. C. Bradley.

As the nineteenth century advanced, the Scottish universities were subject to increasing pressures to conform with developments south of the border, and gradually English standards and methods were imposed on the Scottish system. The age of reform first made itself felt in 1826, when a Royal Commission on the Scottish Universities was set up, and in its report of 1831 advocated a break with tradition and the adoption of more specialized studies. It was chiefly anger at these anglicizing tendencies that provoked Sir William Hamilton's famous attack on Oxford in the *Edinburgh Review*. But the English system of examinations and honours degrees in single subjects gradually found its way into the Scottish universities. A sign of the times was the introduction in 1845 of lectures on the history of English literature, by W. E. Aytoun, the Professor of Rhetoric and Belles Lettres in Edinburgh.[5] Aytoun's predecessor from 1840 to 1845, William Spalding, was now the Professor of Logic, Rhetoric, and Metaphysics at St. Andrews: in an earlier chapter[6] I referred to his *History of English Literature*, published in 1853, as an early example of this new interest in literary history. In 1861 an Executive Commission, appointed by the Universities (Scotland) Act of 1858, drew up new regulations for the ordinary degree of M.A., introducing English as one of the required subjects, alongside Latin, Greek, mathematics, natural philosophy, logic, and moral philosophy. At the same time an honours degree was instituted, though English was not included in the list of subjects from which the student could choose his course. It may be recalled here that the B.A. in English was first created by London University in 1859.

However, the old rhetorical emphasis in English studies was far from being abandoned, as we can see from Professor Aytoun's lecture programme in 1864–5:[7]

1. Lectures in composition.
2. Examination of style as exhibited by the most eminent English authors.
3. The art of public speaking—including the management of the voice and method of delivery.
4. A complete review of British literature ... each epoch being considered referentially to the external history and social development of the country.
5. As the Rhetorical part of the course was strictly practical and useful the Professor 'will not prelect upon the scheme of Formal Rhetoric according to the Aristotelian method, beyond an explanation of its principles. . . . Subsequent to the Christmas recess the Professor will occasionally give elocutionary readings.'

As was the case in England with few exceptions at this date, the historical study of English (or British) literature was as yet separate from the study of criticism, and was consequently little more than an outline of facts and dates about literature. Indeed in 1869 one Scottish professor strongly resisted the suggestion that students needed expert guidance in their understanding of English literature: Alexander Bain, the Professor of Logic at Aberdeen, maintained quite bluntly, in his article 'On Teaching English' in the *Fortnightly Review*, that the study of

[5] G. E. Davie, op. cit., p. 206.   [6] Chapter IV, p. 49, *supra*.
[7] H. W. Meikle, op. cit., p. 102.

Appendix I

literature was worthwhile only as it illustrated the art of composition, which was, he thought, the main concern of the teacher of English:

I hold that an English poet that has not of himself sufficient attraction to be read, understood, and relished, without the prelections of a University professor, is by that very fact a failure. He undertakes to charm the sense and fill the imagination of the ordinary reader, without more effort of study than is repaid on the spot at the moment; his return for any labour expended on him is immediate or nothing. Any special difficulties ensuing from remoteness of age, from the wide scope of his imagery, or from any accidental defects of his composition, may be removed by his elegant and admiring commentator, to be redeemed by his irresistible charms in other respects. If we are to allow a coach in addition to the editor and the review critic, the popular evening lecturer is quite enough. The youthful pupil's forenoon hours are too precious for this kind of work. . . . I could not vote to tax the nation for coaching *Hamlet* and *Macbeth*.

. . . The English teacher's concern with the literature of the past is to extract from it everything that is of value for improving the diction of the pupils, and in that view the present, and not the past, is his mainstay.[8]

One consequence of the changes effected by the Act of 1858, however, was the establishment in 1862 of the Regius Chair of English Language and Literature at Glasgow University. The first Professor was John Nichol, whose references in his Inaugural Lecture to English studies as 'a branch of practical teaching which is of universal utility' veil the fact that he was a teacher of a new stamp. Returning to Scotland after four years at Balliol from 1855 to 1859, he was the first of a succession of professors of English produced by that college, including Churton Collins, W. P. Ker, Henry Sweet, and A. C. Bradley. He taught the critical appreciation of literature, pioneered University Extension in the north from 1866, and was invited by Jowett to deliver two of his courses in Oxford in 1868 and 1869. Apart from his textbooks on literary history, and on English composition, Nichol contributed volumes on *Byron* (1880) and *Carlyle* (1892) to the 'English Men of Letters' series, and wrote studies of *Burns* (1882) and of *Francis Bacon* (2 vols., 1889); furthermore, his article on American literature for the *Encyclopaedia Britannica* in 1882, following a visit to that country in 1865, was an early harbinger of more modern developments in English studies.

Another professor in the modern style was Bain's assistant and his successor at Aberdeen in 1880, William Minto. Like Nichol, Minto had

8 *Fortnightly Review*, Vol. VI, New Series, pp. 211–13.

studied in Oxford, spending a year at Merton College in 1866-7. His interests lay in the eighteenth century, and, like Henry Morley, David Masson, and George Saintsbury, he acquired his experience in writing for the great literary journals of the day. In 1879 his study of *Defoe* was published in the 'English Men of Letters' series, following some humble works designed for students, such as the *Manual of English Prose Literature* (1872), and *Characteristics of the English Poets, Chaucer to Shirley* (1874). But his immense learning and particular interests were most fully embodied in his compendious study of *English Literature under the Georges*, published posthumously in 1894. Nevertheless, the rhetorical tradition lingered in Scotland long after its disappearance from English studies in the south: Minto's successor in Aberdeen, the late Sir Herbert Grierson, had to prepare a course of lectures on composition and style when he left Oxford to take up his duties there in 1893, and we are told that the young Grierson's enthusiasm for Pater was not wholly shared by that dour and conservative community.[9]

But change was advancing rapidly. The Universities (Scotland) Act of 1889 entrusted a new Executive Commission with responsibility for making further reforms, assimilating the Scottish universities ever more closely to the English system; and in 1892 an Ordinance of this Commission extended the choice of subjects for the honours degree of M.A. to include English language and literature. Previously English studies had been confined to the ordinary M.A. on the traditional Scottish model of a general unspecialized education. At Aberdeen the Chair to which Grierson was appointed in 1893 was separated from that of Logic and renamed as the Professorship of English Language and Literature. In 1889 A. C. Bradley had succeeded John Nichol at Glasgow, and in 1895 Saintsbury became Professor at Edinburgh, after David Masson's long reign. In that year, too, David Nichol Smith became the first Edinburgh graduate with First Class Honours in English, a course which his elder brother, Gregory Smith, had largely designed and taught as Masson's assistant. Nothing better illustrates the growing traffic in English studies between both sides of the border than the interest shown in Scotland in the controversies fermented by Churton Collins. In 1891, John Nichol was invited to deliver the session's Opening Address at University College, Liverpool, and he chose to speak about that topical issue, *The Teaching of English Literature in our*

---

[9] H. J. C. Grierson, *Rhetoric and English Composition*, 1944, Preface, p. vi. See also the obituary notice on Grierson by Professor Daiches in *Proceedings of the British Academy*, Vol. XLVI, 1960, pp. 319-32.

Appendix I

Universities and its Relation to Philology. Nichol sided with Collins, and propounded the Arnoldian view that literary standards were threatened in a democratic age, and that therefore it was the responsibility of universities to act as academies in preserving the highest cultural standards. In Glasgow two years before, W. S. McCormick, a lecturer in English at Queen Margaret College for Women, had publicly taken Edward Freeman to task in his address to the college on *English Literature and University Education*. McCormick pointed out the contradiction between Freeman's contempt for the loose subjective criticism found in periodicals and in his implicit approval of each man's right to his own taste. Apart from some later work on the manuscripts of the *Canterbury Tales*, McCormick was lost to English studies in 1901, when he became the Secretary to the Carnegie Trust for the Scottish universities; but his lecture to Queen Margaret College in 1889 contained a succinct and liberal conception of undergraduate English studies. Throughout the nineteenth century, the Scottish universities had faced the crucial problem of balancing their traditional faith in a broad general education with the need to advance academic standards, and McCormick's description of the scope of a modern English School serves as a fitting conclusion to this survey of English studies in Scotland:

. . . we should know more than a little about something. I do not insist that on some one subject our education should be so full as if we were preparing ourselves to profess it as a calling or business of life; but it should at least be thorough enough for us to realize the full difficulties and full meaning of the subject—the height and breadth and depth of it as a whole. We should be so firmly based in its rudiments at least, that standing on that pedestal we can look out on a scope beyond our reach, and follow with our sympathy and appreciation, if not more closely with our understanding, those who have travelled further than we. And this intelligent sympathy once gained would not be confined to one study, but would extend to all.[10]

[10] W. S. McCormick, *Three Lectures on English Literature*, 1889, 'English Literature and University Education', p. 23.

APPENDIX II
THE BOARD OF EDUCATION
REPORT (1921)

THE end of the First World War brought a widespread feeling that the old age was out, and it was time to begin anew. Not least in English studies, there was an urge to take stock of the past, and a general readiness for change. The opportunity for stock-taking was provided in May 1919 by the Board of Education's establishment of a Departmental Committee to report on *The Teaching of English in England*. The initiative in proposing this Report had been taken by the English Association, a society formed in 1906 by two schoolmasters, F. S. Valentine and G. E. S. Coxhead, 'to foster and develop the study of English as an essential element in our national education'. The Board of Education's Departmental Committee comprised fourteen members, under the chairmanship of Sir Henry Newbolt, and including John Bailey, F. S. Boas, C. H. Firth, Sir Arthur Quiller-Couch, Caroline Spurgeon, and, as Secretary, J. Dover Wilson. He was then an inspector of schools, as Matthew Arnold had been, and that influential precedent can be felt in some of the Report's best features. Rarely has the Civil Service produced such a readable document.

However, it is for the most part a rather uncritical acclaim of the prestige of English literature as an educational instrument. Scattered through its 400 pages are reiterated generalizations about the 'glories' of the national literature, and the wide scope of the survey is somewhat flimsily grounded upon vague assumptions about the cultural influence of the subject. As an official Report it is disappointingly nebulous in its conclusions.

Nevertheless the report voiced the general dissatisfaction with outworn methods of teaching which had lingered on in schools and universities since the previous century. It endorsed the criticism of the narrowness of old-fashioned philology in undergraduate courses, and recognized that the study of language should include syntax and semantics as well as phonology, particularly where it is combined with the critical and historical study of literature. Professor Wyld, amongst others, was quoted in support of this view:[1]

[1] *The Teaching of English in England*, 1921, p. 219.

179

He stated that it was 'often supposed that the subject ended with Chaucer, but the problems of Old English were comparatively simple compared with some recent problems from the fifteenth century. The problems were more interesting, more vital, more living, more literary, more human, and really more difficult after Chaucer than before.'

The undue emphasis upon literary history, as a series of facts and dates to be crammed from a textbook at the expense of reading the works themselves, is also justly censured. There is, too, a welcome refutation of the time-honoured theory that education is a process of mental training in which the subject-matter is of value in direct proportion to its difficulty and abstruseness:

A quasi-scientific theory has long been accepted that the process of education is the performance of compulsory hard labour, a 'grind' or 'stiffening process', a 'gritting of the teeth' upon hard substances with the primary object not of acquiring a particular form of skill or knowledge but of giving the mind a general training and strengthening. This theory has now been critically examined and declared to be of less wide application than was thought.[2]

But the Report was less happy in its attempt to make more constructive proposals. Affirming the well-worn but imprecise axiom that education in general should be related more closely to life, the Committee tended to regard English studies as the keystone of an ideal educational framework, and entertained the curious belief that the subject would somehow help to break down the barriers of social class reflected and perpetuated by the contemporary system: shades of Christian Socialism, perhaps. In other words, English studies should rank as the central humane and cultural study for both formal and informal, specialist and general education. This view was never fully formulated in the Report, though it is frequently implied and lay behind many of the Committee's recommendations. It comes closest to articulation in the scheme tentatively put forward by John Bailey:

Would it not be possible for a University into whose scheme it could be fitted, to establish two successive 'Schools' of English intended to follow one upon the other as those of Classical Moderations and Literae Humaniores at Oxford have always done? . . . The suggestion is that there might be established an English Moderations in which the main element was pure literature and the study of the language necessary for its complete understanding; and an English Literae Humaniores in which the history and philosophy of our country were

[2]Op. cit., p. 7.

the principal elements, as the Greek and Roman philosophers and historians are the principal elements of its prototype.[3]

Bailey's admiration for Oxford Greats blinded him to the already distinct character of English studies. When David Nichol Smith was asked to comment on this scheme, he 'offered no opinion on the suggestion, but remarked that the character of the School would be entirely altered and it would no longer be a School of English language and literature'.[4] Cambridge, however, did not accord the idea quite so chill a reception: the English School there had in fact been recently reformed along lines similar to those now advocated by Bailey, and the Committee heard a good deal of evidence from that university, not all of it entirely reassuring. H. M. Chadwick, the Professor of Anglo-Saxon, explained the governing principle of the reformed Tripos:

When Sir Arthur Quiller-Couch and I became Professors in 1912 we had to face the question whether the English Honours School was to continue to be primarily a training for philologists, or whether it ought to change its character and become a course in humane studies—designed primarily for education rather than for special training . . . we hesitated for three years. We knew that if the change was to be made we should have a much larger school. It required no prophet to see that the days of a general classical education were nearly past, and that we should soon have to consider the question which is before us now—viz., whether English is to take the place of Classics.[5]

As I observed earlier, Professor Raleigh scouted the suggestion that English could or should take the place of Greats in Oxford: he wanted his school to attract only those with a genuine capacity for literary studies. Neither did the new Cambridge School escape criticism from some members of the Committee, and one of the Cambridge witnesses, A. J. Wyatt, himself thought that the reformed Tripos was too wide in its scope and permitted students to pass 'without any substantial knowledge of the great English masters later than Shakespeare'.[6] One paper of the Tripos in particular came under fire from the Committee, namely that on 'Literature, Life, and Thought, 1350–1603', which was defended somewhat lamely by the Rev. H. F. Stewart,[7] Chairman of the Board

---

[3] Ibid., p. 206.
[4] Report of Evidence given on 18 March 1920. (A copy was presented to the English Library in Oxford by C. H. Firth, and is used in the following pages.)
[5] Report of Evidence given on 30 April 1920.
[6] Report of Evidence given on 19 February 1920.
[7] Report of Evidence given on 5 March 1920.

of Medieval and Modern Languages which bore the responsibility for altering the old Tripos:

In the period 1350–1603, when literature was still not yet first-rate, literature was strengthened by the introduction of the study of life and thought; but in the period from 1603 onwards, when literature was prominent and glorious, it stood alone.

This paper was thus a test-case for the movement to convert English studies into a general School of National Culture, such as Bailey and some of the Cambridge witnesses envisaged. But when Professor Quiller-Couch was himself put on the witness-stand and challenged by his Committee-colleague, F. S. Boas, he did not defend his case very convincingly:[8]

Dr. Boas said that he could not regard a paper which contained no question on the drama, while it included questions on the guild system and the development of the merchant class, as a properly-balanced English Literature paper.

Sir Arthur Quiller-Couch answered that the Tripos was an 'English Tripos' not limited to English Language and Literature: he added that the examination in 1919 was the first under the new regulations and there were special reasons why insufficient consultation between the examiners took place. He did not see the papers in time to make all the alterations he would have wished. . . . The reason why History only extended to 1603 was because for the purpose of understanding the subsequent literature a knowledge of the social life of the time was not needed to anything like the same extent that it was needed in order to understand say Chaucer.

There is a similar feebleness in the evasive reply of 'Q' to the criticism that the amount of literature included in the syllabus was insufficient: 'a man was not a graduate in language or in literature, but M.A. of Cambridge University'.

The discussion of John Bailey's scheme and of the reformed Cambridge Tripos brings out very clearly the different lines on which English studies were progressing in the two ancient universities, and it must be said that the kind of arguments heard from Cambridge could scarcely have inspired confidence in their experiment. Perhaps they did not make the best of their case, since the attitude to English studies as the basis of a broad moral and cultural education, a modern 'Classics', was as old as the subject itself; though it was more frequently related to popular education than to centres of learning as venerable as Cam-

[8] Report of Evidence given on 4 March 1920.

bridge. The Report itself is if anything more in sympathy with the old idea of literary missionaries among the cultural slums than with the advancement of English studies in the academic world. Reading the Report today, one is impressed chiefly by its pervading optimism and idealism, perhaps a post-war reaction rather than mere nebulous high-mindedness: 'the rise of modern Universities has accredited an ambassador of poetry to every important capital of industrialism in the country', it grandly proclaimed.[9]

Moreover, though the Report is seldom positive in its proposals, the desire to promote English studies as a general broadly-conceived cultural education, rather than as a specialist training, resulted in a certain unfairness towards the position of Old and Middle English. A considerable number of witnesses complained of the narrow spirit in which early literature was often studied, but the Committee also heard evidence, from the same witnesses in Oxford and elsewhere, affirming that a study of the earlier language and literature was essential to reflect the continuity of the subject. Nevertheless the report recommended that Old and Middle English should not be compulsory subjects in university departments, but should rather be made alternatives to medieval Latin or French. R. W. Chambers found these suggestions unacceptable, and promptly rose to the defence of medieval English. In a pamphlet published by the English Association in July 1922, *The Teaching of English in the Universities of England*,[10] he argued that in all English universities by one means or another students of English were already required to possess a competent knowledge of Latin and French, and that it was therefore unnecessary, to say the least, to oust early English in favour of other medieval languages. In 1923 Chambers succeeded W. P. Ker as Professor at University College, London, and his Inaugural Lecture, *Concerning Certain Great Teachers of the English Language*, was a further criticism of the Report's readiness to condemn the work of English philologists as 'German' (the newly-defeated enemy). Chambers gave a more sympathetic account of Henry Morley, John Earle, and Walter Skeat, and showed their scholarship to have been more humane and less narrow than the impression of it conveyed by the Report. He also took the opportunity to point out, however gently, that several members of the Committee, including John Bailey, the originator of the English 'Greats' scheme, themselves lacked any experience of the teaching of English.

---

[9] *The Teaching of English in England*, p. 259.
[10] *English Association Pamphlet No. 53.*

Appendix II

The same criticism could have been made of the English Association generally, which was beginning to forget the strictly professional character of its foundation, in widening the scope of its leadership and social activities towards the cultivation of literary personalities and genteel amateurism. Reflecting in 1942 on *The Origins and History of the Association*, Nowell Smith frankly confessed in his Chairman's Address that

I do not think it can be gainsaid that from about the time of the last war the attention paid by the Executive and the leaders of the Association to the work among and for the teachers in the schools tended to relax. It was as if the publication of that Report on *The Teaching of English* in 1921 was so fine a flower as to exhaust the tree planted by Valentine and Coxhead in 1906.

Nevertheless, the various journals sponsored by the English Association, including *The Year's Work in English Studies*, *Essays and Studies*, and *English*, continued to provide contributions of permanent value, while the Association's pamphlets provided a forum for the airing of new ideas about the methods and spirit of English studies. I have just referred to the pamphlet written by R. W. Chambers in 1922; another and more controversial thesis was propounded by the bibliographical scholar, R. B. McKerrow, in his pamphlet published by the Association in June 1921, shortly before the Report appeared.[11] Despite his deceptively modest title, *A Note on the Teaching of 'English Language and Literature'*, *with some Suggestions*, the reforms he was advocating were so thoroughgoing that the Publications Sub-Committee of the Association felt obliged to print a Note disclaiming any responsibility for the views which followed.

McKerrow accepted the premise that, 'whether we like it or not', English was taking the place of Classics in education. The subject therefore needed fortifying to become as valuable an instrument as that which it was replacing. He recommended that the university course in English should have two parts, one elementary, the other more advanced. In the first part, the history of the language should be studied through texts recast into a phonetic alphabet: a proposal based on the arbitrary notion that language is speech, and spelling therefore only a more or less (certainly less in early English literature) efficient method of recording it. The history of English literature, he went on, could no be studied properly unless the student possessed a knowledge of Latin and Greek literature.

[11] *English Association Pamphlet No. 49.*

It is not in the least essential that he should read them in the original, but a student to whom Virgil, Cicero, Ovid, Terence, Juvenal, and Horace (he should probably include Pliny the Elder and Plautus) are no more than names cannot hope to attain a real understanding of modern literature. With Greek the case is rather different: it is mainly the lesser men such as Plutarch and Diogenes Laertius of whom a knowledge is required.

The force of the old argument is undeniable, but McKerrow's implication is that the university course should be only a preparation for the reading of English literature, and that the study of 'background' should take the place of the literary works themselves:

If instead of taking literature by itself we study it as a manifestation of something greater; if we can make clear to our students that thus and thus did the thought of Europe change, and thus and thus is the change shown in its literature, we are genuinely teaching something: we are, indeed, teaching them that most valuable of all ideas, namely the possibility of different outlooks upon life.

It is, in fact, the 'history of ideas' that McKerrow would have us study in literature. He did not give much attention to literary criticism; that was a supplementary factor, dependent upon the teacher.

So much for the elementary part of the course. McKerrow is not very specific as to whether the more advanced study was intended for undergraduates, or as a training for research. But the emphasis in this second phase was to be placed upon the study of the transmission of the texts, upon bibliographical methods and textual criticism. Though McKerrow does not explicitly define the scope of this subject, it was of course mainly in the study of Shakespeare that undergraduates came into contact with bibliography. Even Sir Walter Raleigh, no specialist himself, had recommended to the Board of Education's Committee that 'Honours students of Shakespeare must know how Shakespeare's works were first given to the world'. McKerrow's plan seems to go considerably beyond this modest requirement, however.

Of all the strange ideas fermenting in this post-war period, McKerrow's are by far the most startling, but not all of them have fallen on stony ground, as I hope this book has shown.

To this science of textual criticism must certainly be joined a sketch of the historical development of the study of our language and literature, and this not as a means of commemorating those who have been before us, but for the purpose of criticizing their methods, and evaluating their statements.

INDEX

Aberdeen, University of, 171, 177
Academy, 106
Accidence, 4, 10
Act of Toleration (1689), 7
Act of Uniformity (1662), 7
Addison, J., 8, 9, 26
Adult Education: spread of literacy, 29–31; Mechanics' Institutes, 31–33; their continuing with University Extension classes, 32, 34; Working Men's College, 35–38; English studies in Extension Lectures, 53, 55; their influence on ancient universities, 56, 66, 81, 93–94, 96–97, 119, 176; their connection with 'civic' universities, 61, 63, 183 (*see also* Women's Education)
Aikin, J., 7–8
Akenside, M., 8
American literature, 163, 176
American universities, 117, 163, 167
Anglo-Saxon studies; literary value, 24; at University College London, 25, 28; teaching of Anglo-Saxon, 62, 63, 183; in Oxford, 71–76, 87, 141, 156–7; nineteenth-century status, 76 (*see also* Philology)
Appleton, H. W., 62
Arber, E., 62–63, 143
Armstrong, E., 100
Arnold, M., 30, 47–48, 64, 82, 91–92, 95, 178, 179
Arnold, T., 41–43
Ascham, R., 3
Aytoun, W. E., 175

Bacon, Francis, 5–6, 7, 15, 49–50, 176
Bailey, J., 179, 180–2, 184
Bain, A., 175–6
Ballad Society, 38
Barbauld, Mrs. L., 8
Barnett, P. A., 61
Bayley, R. S., 35
Belfour, A. O., 134, 140
Bell, John, 34

Belles Lettres, 7–9, 11, 15, 22, 171–5
Bentham, J., 18–19, 67
Bible, The, 8, 30
Bibliography, the 'new bibliography', 50, 142
Birmingham, University of, 56, 62–63, 132
Blair, A., 25
Blair, H., 11–12, 24, 33, 173–4
Board of Education, 152 (*see also* Appendix II)
Boas, F. S., 179, 182
Bolingbroke, Lord, 8
Bowring, T., 18–19
Boyer, James (Christ's Hospital), 43
Bradley, A. C., 62, 64, 79, 82, 120, 122, 123, 130, 174, 176, 177
Bradley, Rev. G. G. (Marlborough School), 44
Bradshaw, H., 38
Brathwaite, R., *English Gentleman* (1630), 10
Brett-Smith, H. F. B., 134
Brewer, J. S., 54
Brinsley, J., *Ludus Literarius* (1627), 5, 10
Brooke, Rupert, 158
Brougham, H., 16, 31
Brown, A., 174
Bunyan, John, 30
Burke, Edmund, 36
Butler, Samuel, 26
Byron, Lord, 23, 53, 176
Bywater, I., 111, 130

Cambridge, University of: Tripos in Medieval and Modern Languages (1878), 80, 87, 95, 103, 111, 151; development of English School, 149, 151–8, 181–2; 'Life, Literature, and Thought', 152, 153, 155–6, 159, 181–2; practical criticism, 152, 154–5 (*see also* Chadwick, H. M.; Quiller-Couch, A.; Tillyard, E. M. W.; Leavis, F. R.)
Carlyle, T., 19, 176
Case, T., 100, 109, 112, 121
Cassell, John, 34, 50

187

Index

Castiglione, B., 10

Chadwick, H. M., 152–3, 181

Chambers, Robert, *Cyclopaedia of English Literature* (1844), 34, 48

Chambers, R. W., 183–4

Chambers, William, 34

Chartism, 33, 35

Chaucer, Geoffrey, 2, 23, 27, 34, 37, 51, 113, 128, 139, 143, 147, 177

Chaucer Society, 38

Chesterfield, Lord, 9

Christian Socialism, 35, 63, 180 (*see also* Maurice, Rev. F. D.; Kingsley, Rev. C.)

Civic Universities, *see under separate universities*

Civil Service, 46, 49, 62, 81, 90, 179

Civil War, 6

Clare, John, 34

Clarendon, Lord, 22

Clarendon Press, 50, 125

Clark, W. G., 49

Clarke, Cowden, 33

Classical authors: Aeschylus, 83; Aristotle, 4; Cicero, 3, 5, 84, 185; Diogenes Laertius, 185; Horace, 84, 185; Juvenal, 185; Ovid, 185; Persius, 11; Pindar, 84; Plato, 84; Plutarch, 185; Plautus, 185; Pliny the Elder, 185; Sophocles, 83, 84; Terence, 3, 185; Virgil, 185

Classics: school curriculum in sixteenth and seventeenth centuries, 2–4; supplemented in Dissenting Academies, 7; model for English studies, 11, 41–46, 81–87, 180–1; educational advantages over vernacular, 12, 41; a literary education, 13; Professors of English trained in, 62–63, 64; supremacy at Oxford, 77–79; need to relate English studies to, 81–87, 91–92, 104, 153, 163; English studies supplanting, 83, 158, 184–5 (*see also* Oxford: Greats (*Lit. Hum.*) and Classical Mods.)

Cleland, J., *Institution of a Young Nobleman* (1607), 10

Clough, A. H., 27, 51

Coleridge, S. T., 40, 43, 159

Colet, Dean, 3, 4

Collins, J. C., 64, 65, 79, 80–99, 104, 112, 130, 133, 142, 151, 152, 176, 178

Comenius, 6

Comparative literature, 163

Contemporary Review, 98–100

Cooke, John, 34

Cooper, T., 33–34.

Copleston, E., 68

Coulton, G. C., 153

Cowley, Abraham, 26

Craigie, W. J., 107, 144

Craik, G. C., *Sketches of Literature and Learning in England* (1844), 48

Dale, Rev. T., 18–25, 28, 37, 52

Dalzel, Andrew, 43

Dasent, G. W., 46–47, 54

Daventry Academy, 8

Defoe, D., 7, 53, 177

Degree structures, 161–5, 172, 174 (*see also under separate universities*)

Dekker, Thomas, 25, 53

de Selincourt, E., 64, 115, 116, 130, 132–3

Dickens, Charles, 33, 50, 88

Dictionary of National Biography, 8, 143

Dissenters, 7

Dissenting Academies, 7–9, 16

Dobson, Austin, *Civil Service Handbook of English Literature* (1874), 49

Doddridge, P., 7, 8

Donne, John, 26, 153

Dover Wilson, J., *see* Wilson, J. D.

Dowden, E., 79, 91

Drayton, Michael, 88

Dryden, J., 11, 51, 53, 84, 113

Durham, University of (including New-castle), 63–64, 133

Earle, J., 71–72, 76, 79, 107, 112, 116, 183

Early English Texts Society, 38

Edgeworth, R. L., *Essays on Professional Education* (1809), 68

Edinburgh Review, 68, 174

Edinburgh, University of, 51, 55, 121, 171, 172–4, 175, 177

Editions of English Literature, 2, 30, 34–35, 49–50, 62–63, 73–76, 81, 106, 121, 126, 141, 142, 153

Elegant Extracts, 13

Eliot, T. S., 154, 155, 158

Ellershaw, H., 63

Elstob, E., 74–75

Elstob, W., 74

Elton, O., 64

Elyot, Sir T., 2, 10

Enfield, W., 8–9

English Association, 179, 183, 184

English studies, their nature and purpose: the vernacular in seventeenth-century education, 4–5; English more useful than

188

Index

Index

Lee, Nathaniel, 26
Leeds, University of (Yorkshire College), 56, 59, 60–62, 143
Leicester, University of, 32
Lewis, C. S., 169, 170
Lily, W., High Master of St. Paul's School, Latin *Grammar*, 3, 4
Linguistics, 163
Liverpool, University College, 56, 59, 62, 120, 141, 178
Llewelyn Davies, J., 36
Locke, J., 4, 9, 15, 53
London, University of: 16–17, 37, 47; University College: foundation, 16–18; early professors of English, 25–27, 28, 50; King's College: foundation, 16–18; early professors of English, 27–28, 36, 50, 53–54; Birkbeck College, 32; Bedford College, 54 (*see also* Dale, Rev. T.; Maurice, Rev. F. D.; Morley, H.)
Low's Educational Catalogue, 50
Lytton, Bulwer, 23

Macaulay, T. B., 46, 48, 119
Macmillans (Publishers), 49; *Macmillan's Magazine*, 45
Mallet, D., 26
Manchester, University of (Owens College), 27, 56–60, 79, 119, 124, 171; Victoria University, 59, 61
Mandeville, Sir John, 23
Marshall, W., 73
Marston, Rev. H. J. R., 63
Marvell, Andrew, 26
Masson, D., 27, 50, 51, 55, 59, 122, 171, 177
Maurice, Rev. F. D., 27–28, 35, 47, 52, 55
Max Müller, F., 76, 95, 107, 115, 124, 125
McCormick, W. S., 178
McKerrow, R. B., 142, 184–6
Meres, F., 1
Methodism, *see* Wesleyanism
Middle English, 113, 115, 128, 139, 145–6, 152 (*see also* Anglo-Saxon; Philology)
Mill, J. S., 39
Milton, John, 6, 8, 27, 30, 33, 37, 46, 81, 84, 106, 113, 120, 126, 129
Minto, W., 177
Modern Languages, 7, 95, 110
Moir, G., 174
Monro, D. B., 96, 107, 111, 113
Moore, G. E., 154
Moore Smith, G. C., 35, 62

Morley, H., 50–53, 55, 59, 62, 118, 122, 177, 183
Morley, J., 91, 93–94
Morris, William, 63
Mulcaster, R., *The First Part of the Elementarie* (1582), 4
Müller, Max, *see* Max Müller

Napier, A. S., 79–80, 82, 107, 112, 113, 115, 124, 128–9, 130, 137, 139, 141, 143–4
Nettleship, H., 102, 104–6
Nettleship, R. L., 71, 82–83, 107
Newbolt, Sir H., 179
Newington Green Academy, 7
Newman, J. H., 17
New Shakespere Society, 38
Newton, I., 4
Nichol, J., 64, 176–7, 178
Nichol Smith, D., 121, 127, 130, 131, 133, 137, 144, 150, 167, 177, 181
Nicholson, William, 74
Northampton Academy, 7, 16
North Staffs., University of, 161
Nottingham, University College, 32, 55–56, 63, 66

Onions, C. T., 148
Otway, T., 26
Oxford and Cambridge Local Examinations (1858), 47
Oxford Magazine, 90, 92–93, 143
Oxford, University of: Greats (*Lit. Hum.*) and Classical Mods., 64, 67, 77, 101, 109, 112, 139, 149, 153, 157, 159, 163, 164, 181; university reform, 66–72, 77, 78–79; conflict of professorial with college interests, 69, 77, 78–79, 83, 87, 131, 134, 150; Hebdomadal Council, 69–70, 93, 107, 108–9, 132, 145; Congregation, 70, 95–96, 102–3, 104, 107, 110, 111, 122, 132, 136–7; School of Modern History, 70–71, 95, 101, 109, 149; early Anglo-Saxon studies in Oxford, 71–76; Rawlinson and Bosworth Professorship of Anglo-Saxon, 71, 75, 107, 112, 144; Professorship of Comparative Philology, 76, 124, 141; Merton Professorship of English Language and Literature, 79–80, 98, 107, 112, 144, 145; Professorship of Poetry, 95, 107, 133; Modern Languages Statute (1887), 95–103, 107; Statute establishing English School, 111–12; Merton Professorship of English Literature, 112, 144

Index

Index

Sheffield, University of (Firth College), 56, 126

Shelley, P. B., 36, 41

Sheridan, T., 5, 9

Sidgwick, A., 97, 107, 136

Sidney, Sir Philip, 2, 88

Simpson, P., 127, 142, 143, 148

Skeat, W. W., 125, 153, 183

Smith, Adam, 173

Smith, D. Nichol, *see* Nichol Smith, D.

Society for the Diffusion of Useful Knowledge, 34

Somner, W., 73

Southey, R., 27, 67

Spalding, W., 49, 175

Speght, T., edition of Chaucer (1598), 2

Spelman, Henry, 73

Spenser, Edmund, 2, 49, 51, 157

Spurgeon, C., 179

Steam Press, 35

Stewart, Rev. H. F., 182

Stuart, James, 55

Stubbs, W., 71

Sweet, H., 116, 141–2, 176

Swift, Jonathan, 8

Swinburne, A. C., 38, 81, 89–90

Symes, Rev. J. E., 63

Symonds, J. A., 89, 91–92

Taylor, T., 26

Tennyson, Alfred Lord, 37, 38, 46, 84, 89

The Times, 96, 117

Thomson, J., 8

Thorpe, B., 76

Thwaites, E., 74

Tiddy, R. J. E., 133, 134, 136, 137, 148

Tillyard, E. M. W., 151, 152, 153, 154

Toller, T. N., 59

Trivium, 2

Tyndale, W., 2

Utilitarianism, 5–6, 7, 9, 13, 15–17, 28

Vives, 4

Wanley, H., 74–76

Ward, A. W., 59, 119, 122

Warren, T. H., 122, 144

Warrington Academy, 8

Watson, R., 173

Wesley, C., 30

Wesleyanism, 15, 30

Wheloc, Abraham, 73

Whole Duty of Man, The, 10

Willey, B., 153

Wilson, F. P., 133, 142

Wilson, J. D., 179

Women's Education: suitability of English studies for women, 38–39, 111; Oxford Association for the Higher Education of Women (1878), 56, 97, 125, 126; women admitted to Owens College (1883), 58; women in Oxford English School, 116, 137 (*see also* Oxford English School: numerical strength)

Wordsworth, W., 17, 18, 36, 41, 53, 84, 121, 129, 157

Wright, J., 124–6, 128, 130, 131, 134, 137, 139, 143, 144, 145

Wright, W. A., 49–50

Wyatt, A. J., 181

Wycliffe, J., 23

Wyld, H. C. K., 141, 144, 147, 179–80

York Powell, F., 97, 102, 107, 113, 122, 126

Young, E., 8

Young, John, 42–43